THE MAGIC LANTERN OF
MARCEL PROUST

THE MAGIC LANTERN OF
MARCEL PROUST

A CRITICAL STUDY OF
Remembrance of Things Past

HOWARD MOSS
Foreword by Damion Searls

PAUL DRY BOOKS
Philadelphia 2012

First Paul Dry Books Edition, 2012

Paul Dry Books, Inc.
Philadelphia, Pennsylvania
www.pauldrybooks.com

Printed in the United States of America

Library of Congress Cataloging-in-Publication Data

Moss, Howard, 1922–1987.
  The magic lantern of Marcel Proust : a critical study of
Remembrance of things past / Howard Moss ; foreword by
Damion Searls. — 1st Paul Dry Books ed.
     p. cm.
  ISBN 978-1-58988-079-5 (pbk.)
  1. Proust, Marcel, 1871–1922. À la recherche du temps
perdu. I. Title.
  PQ2631.R63A84 2012
  843'.912—dc23

                                        2012026101

For Elizabeth Bowen

This book quotes *Remembrance of Things Past*, the original English translation of Proust's *A la Recherche du temps perdu* by C. K. Scott Moncrieff with the last volume translated by Frederick A. Blossom. (The Scott Moncrieff translation and a translation by Andreas Mayor of the last volume were later revised by Terence Kilmartin for the three-volume black-and-silver Vintage edition, then revised again by D. J. Enright for the six-volume gold-spine Modern Library edition retitled *In Search of Lost Time*.)

Citations in this book indicate the English titles of each volume, given below with their original French equivalents; where the English-language volume published by Random House is divided into two sections, Roman numerals indicate the section. Arabic numerals indicate the page.

SW: *Swann's Way* (*Du Côté de chez Swann*)
WBG I and II: *Within a Budding Grove* (*A l'Ombre des jeunes filles en fleurs*)
GW I and II: *The Guermantes Way* (*Le Côté de Guermantes*)
CP I and II: *Cities of the Plain* (*Sodome et Gomorrhe*)
C I and II: *The Captive* (*La Prisonnière*)
SCG: *The Sweet Cheat Gone* (*Albertine disparue*) [called *The Fugitive* in later translations]
PR: *The Past Recaptured* (*Le Temps retrouvé*) [called *Time Regained* in later translations]

CONTENTS

FOREWORD

Damion Searls

Of all the big classic books in modern literature, *Remembrance of Things Past* is probably the least in need of explanation. There is no code external to the book, like the Homeric references in *Ulysses* or the intellectual history behind *The Magic Mountain*; there are not many main characters, certainly compared to *Gravity's Rainbow* or *A Dance to the Music of Time*; all of the political and historical background, from Racine to the Dreyfus Case, is sufficiently explained in the book itself. In fact, if there is one thing Proust likes to do it's explain. He is only too happy to stop and analyze every possible nuance of whatever it is, whether that means thirty-one pages on the reasons why Princesse de Parme is nice to the narrator at the Duchesse de Guermantes's dinner party (ten pages on the first reason, twenty-one on the second) or close to a thousand on the workings of jealousy. Everything there is to say—more than any critic would have the genius to unpack—is right there in the book.

This has not prevented a mountain of studies from being written about Proust's masterpiece, of course, but they all simply set out from whichever aspect of Proust's universe sparks the critic's interest. Like no other writer before or since (Dante and Nabokov at his best come close), Proust is fractal, as it were, with the whole vast structure implicit in every chapter, paragraph, sentence. You can start anywhere—at Impressionism or lesbianism, asthma or memory, architecture or etymology, Jewishness or fashion, war or hawthorns—and it will be no less central to Proust than anything else. How good the resulting book of criticism is depends more on its author than its topic.

Howard Moss's slim and masterful *The Magic Lantern of Marcel Proust* is in some ways an exception, because it has no special topic at all, no theory to prove or argument to make. It synthesizes or distills the whole of Proust's massive work, condensing without reducing or simplifying. Moss lays out the sweeping claims and overarching structure of *Remembrance of Things Past*—the significance of Swann's Way and the Guermantes Way, or why there are such long party scenes—and is equally good at bringing to light all kinds of tiny, revealing details: The "magic potion" of the madeleine dipped in tea is "a tiny garden image in itself, for the tea consists of lime blossoms steeped in water"; the colors of Marcel's first glimpse of the Duchesse de Guermantes recapitulate the colors of his childhood magic lantern; all the scenes the narrator spies through windows are the key to his voyeuristic sexual psychology.

Among the many admirers of Moss's book, both John Updike and Elizabeth Bishop reserved special praise for its discussion of habit and memory in chapter 5. (Updike rightly called it "truly wonderful—wonderful as explication, as psychology, and as philosophy.") For me, the most sublime moment in the book comes near the end, when Moss lets us see *Remembrance of Things Past* as not just a cathedral (a common cliché in describing Proust) but a kind of four-dimensional cathedral, which "derives its energy from the epochs of time that have seeped into its very cells." Any piece of social or physical reality that we come to understand refutes and defeats our understanding soon enough, because that reality changes over time, and also because we change in time, so that our relation to that reality changes. This sensitivity to shifts and reconfigurations is what makes Proust's writing, analytical as it is, so alive ("It remained dark. The balcony in front of the window was grey. Suddenly, on its sullen stone, I would not exactly see a less leaden colour, but I would feel as it were a striving towards a less leaden colour, the pulsation of a hesitant ray that struggled to discharge its light. A moment later, the balcony was as pale and luminous as a pool at dawn, and a thousand shadows from the iron-work of its balustrade had alighted on it"). Moss notices all sorts of patterns in Proust but keeps them as mobile and fleeting as Proust has made them.

In a later essay, Moss wrote that "Both Chekhov and Proust had a firm grip on reality and both were absolutely truthful. Proust analyzes and concludes. Chekhov presents and reveals." Moss notices and reminds. He is more like Chekhov, though his firm grip here is on a book, not on life. There is no mention in *The Magic Lantern* of biographical facts—Proust's being gay, or rich, or half-Jewish, or often sick; you would not know from this book that Proust left *Remembrance of Things Past* unfinished, or that he published *Swann's Way* as the first volume of a projected trilogy before the war years gave him the time and the impetus to double its length. Moss never brings up any issues of translation from the French. He simply takes the book as it comes, as it is for us—seven English-language volumes full of immeasurable riches. He reads the book because the book is worth reading, and because he is so very good at reading it. And when we in turn read Moss, he does not make us think about static literary structures, but sets us dreaming about life itself—one of the finest accomplishments of any critic.

The Magic Lantern of Marcel Proust feels old-fashioned, but not in a bad way—or rather, only in a way that reflects badly on our current fashions, not on the book. Unlike most recent writers on Proust, Moss assumes that we have actually read *Remembrance of Things Past* and anticipates (and conduces to) our reading it again. He has no qualms about giving away crucial plot points or spoiling surprises; he does not pander in the least to anyone who might claim to have no time in his or her busy life to read a four-thousand-page novel. He wrote in an age when high culture was not just the passkey to an academic confraternity or the object of a lone individual's quest to find and join the tradition, but a shared heritage; Saul Bellow mentions in several novels written after Moss's book how lawyers used to have to have read Proust, dentists were expected to have opinions on Stendhal. Moss's book was part of the culture's collective effort to sustain that heritage. He aimed neither to supplant Proust's book nor to supplement it but to enhance it and our appreciation of it.

Howard Moss opened his introduction to a 1959 Keats anthology as follows: "When a poet becomes a legend, his poems are obscured; the man becomes more important than his works. Keats was particularly unfortunate in this respect." Moss was particularly fortunate in this respect. We have now reached the point in the introduction where biographical information is to be supplied, but I find myself reluctant to supply it. Moss had as much of a biography as anyone else, of course, but what seems to matter here are three dates and one job: he was born in 1922, joined the *New Yorker* in 1948, and worked there as the poetry editor until his death in 1987.

He was a poet as well as an editor—his *Selected Poems* won the National Book Award in 1972—and he considered himself a poet first, resenting the demands of his job upon both his time and his social universe. (He never knew, for most of his life, whether people were honestly being nice to him or just trying to get in good with the poetry editor of the *New Yorker*.) But his poetry has not held up well, in my view; it has that well-polished mid-century blandness about it—Merrill without the virtuosity, Merwin without the tenacity, Bishop without the utter genius. In any case, *The Magic Lantern of Marcel Proust*, with all its brilliant perceptiveness and crystal-clear writing, is an editor's book more than a poet's book. Moss is fully willing to subordinate, and devote, his own talent and vision to another author's. This sounds like damning with faint praise, especially in the context of today's values, but I mean it as a high compliment: he was working in the service of Proust and a world that reads Proust. Moss reminds me of what Calvino once wrote about his own long-standing job in the culture industry: "Working in a publishing house, I spent more time with the books of others than with my own. I do not regret it: everything that is useful to the whole business of living together in a civilized way is energy well spent."

Moss was at the center of a vibrant American literary culture for forty years, and lives on in the culture today. He gets several warm mentions in Nicholson Baker's great 2009 novel *The Anthologist*: "Moss was in his lovely self-effacing way a genius. You could hear notes of Wallace Stevens in him, and sometimes Bishop, and sometimes even Auden, but he was able to give it his own sad, affectionate jostle. . . . Ginsberg was over here, going 'first thought best thought, first thought best thought,' and Howard Moss was over here, quietly watching the sun go down through his ice cubes after a day at the office writing a letter accepting a poem sent in by Elizabeth Bishop." Those letters to and from Bishop have recently been published too, in *Elizabeth Bishop and The New Yorker: The Complete Correspondence* (2011), and they paint a fine picture of Moss's sensibility, kindness, and culture. Now, fifty years after its publication in 1962, Moss's book about Proust is back in print, doing its noble part in the whole business of living together in a civilized way.

THE MAGIC LANTERN OF
MARCEL PROUST

I

THE TWO WAYS

Everything, indeed, is at least twofold. (SCG 362)

Remembrance of Things Past is more than a novel; it is a work in which a single person's life is transformed into a mythology, with its own pantheon of gods, its own religious rituals, and its own moral laws. A total vision, it does not rely on any system outside itself for support. It is as if Dante had set out to write the *Paradiso* and the *Inferno* utilizing only the facts of his own existence without any reference to Christianity. Marcel, the narrator, has his equivalent of Vergil—Swann. But Swann's significance is created by Proust and is not historical. With Proust, we are in the presence of a unique being—not someone who is transcribing a reality created by God, but one who is a god himself. Other novelists describe or invent worlds. *Remembrance of Things Past* is an entire universe created and interpreted by Marcel Proust.

It is the story of how a little boy becomes a writer. That is the first—and last—simple statement that can be made about it. A truer definition is impossibly complicated: it is the biography of a novelist written by its subject, who has decided to write a novel instead of an autobiography, and whose only novel is the biography he is writing. A book in which real people, natural objects, and institutions appear, yet resorting, like a fairy tale, to deception to reach the truth, *Remembrance of Things Past* is a house of mirrors. Scenes are mapped out and actions take place. Resembling a novel, it is not what the French would call a *roman* or what we would call a "story," and uniquely combines the qualities of the epic and the lyric. Though its characters end up as heroes, it is completely metaphorical. It is the first epic ever written whose battles are mostly internal; yet those battles are merely the minor actions in a gigantic poem. Proust put everything he knew into it—a mistake made only by amateur writers and very great ones. The narrator of Proust's novel is named Marcel, but he is not Proust. And that is where the deception begins.

In the original complication of having the narrator and the author of *Remembrance of Things Past* bear the same Christian name, Proust begins the process of merging appearance and reality in order that he may, ultimately, separate them. This doubling of names makes us aware that we are reading a novel that is, in some way, based on fact; it warns us simultaneously that appearances can be deceiving. This strange

duality, connecting and yet severing the "I" of the
book from the "I" of its creator, suggests its theme:
It is nothing less than the rescuing of the self from
the oblivion of time. There is an "I" that needs to be
rescued; there is an "I" that does the rescuing. Inso-
far as each successfully acts out this role, the "Marcel" of Proust's narrator more cleverly disguises himself than any other name possibly could. The fictional
Marcel becomes aware of the need of salvation only as
he turns into the Marcel who creates him. And it is in
the process of that creation that salvation exists. It is a
difficult and all-important strategy. At the same time
as this duality foreshadows the theme of the novel, another duality becomes the basic structural device of
the work.

As a child, Marcel spends his Easter vacations at his
Aunt Léonie's country house in Combray. Her house
is so situated that doors on opposite sides lead to one
or the other of two "ways"—two mutually exclusive
walks that Marcel may take into the countryside. One
of these ways is the "Méséglise way," where Swann's
house, Tansonville, is located, and where Marcel first
sees Swann's daughter, Gilberte, when they are both
young. The other way is the "Guermantes way," the
domain of the Guermantes family, the feudal sov-
ereigns of Combray and the neighboring districts
ever since the Middle Ages. The Méséglise way—or
Swann's way—is a plain. The Guermantes way is river
land. Both these ways are real, but share, in common,

an ideality which, because of the peculiar time scheme of Proust's novel, is the product of memory and anticipation acting together:

> . . . during the whole of my boyhood, if Méséglise was to me something as inaccessible as the horizon, which remained hidden from sight, however far one went, by the folds of a country which no longer bore the least resemblance to the country round Combray, Guermantes, on the other hand, meant no more than the ultimate goal, ideal rather than real, of the "Guermantes way," a sort of abstract geographical term like the North Pole or the Equator. And so to "take the Guermantes way" in order to get to Méséglise, or vice versa, would have seemed to me as nonsensical a proceeding as to turn east in order to reach the west. Since my father used always to speak of the "Méséglise way" as comprising the finest view of a plain that he knew anywhere, and of the "Guermantes way" as typical of river scenery, I had invested each of them, by conceiving them in this way as two distinct entities, with that cohesion, that unity which belongs only to figments of the mind . . . I set between them, far more distinctly than the mere distance in miles and yards and inches which separated one from the other, the distance that there was between the two parts of my brain, in which I used to think of them, one of those distances of the mind which time serves only to lengthen, which separates things irremediably from one another, keeping them forever upon different planes. (SW 191–192)

The word "way" in English, like the phrase *du côté* in French, has a double meaning. It means, on the one hand, a direction, progression, or journey; and on the other, an aspect, manner, or style. "Swann's way" and the "Guermantes way" are pilgrimages and places; they are also modes of living.

In the course of the book, two sets of characters, two different "stories" are associated with each of these ways. The first, the Méséglise, is dominated by Swann, the rich son of a Jewish stockbroker. Swann is a sensitive dilettante, a man of fashion, and an intimate of royalty and aristocracy. The second, the Guermantes, is the world of the Duchesse de Guermantes, and, ultimately, two other Guermantes: the Baron de Charlus, her cousin and brother-in-law, and Robert de Saint-Loup, her nephew. The Guermantes family are aristocracy itself; in many cases, its members, through birth and the inheritance of titles, are the social superiors of European royalty.

These two ways become, in time, two visions of life's possibilities. One is biological—love. The other is social—society. Each falls under the domination of the differentiated "gods" of Marcel's boyhood. Swann's way is the way of love; the Duchesse de Guermantes' that of society. The crossbreeding between them is richly complicated, but they are perceived by Marcel, as a boy, as two distinct forces of life. And, as such, they become complementary themes in the book.

As in most novels, these possibilities are developed through the gradual revelation of character and through the characters' interrelating and conflicting actions. But unlike most novels, each way is associated with major metaphors that proliferate as the novel proceeds. The love, or biological theme, is enveloped in the metaphor of the garden, with its two attendant images, flowers and water. The social theme materializes in the concept of a "party"—in its literal sense of a gathering together of people, as well as its political sense, a group held together by common interests, or committed to an *idée fixe*. Thus the Dreyfus case, the major political scandal of *Remembrance of Things Past*, can be considered in the same sense as an evening soirée at the Princesse de Guermantes; an implicit social ethic is revealed by the behavior of the participants in both cases.

In the "Overture" to *Swann's Way*, Aunt Léonie's house provides the first garden as well as the first party—the family dinner Marcel's parents give at which Swann is the single guest. This intimate dinner is followed by a series of parties and receptions at which most of the social life in Proust's novel takes place. Proust places these metaphors and ideas in his "Overture" in the same way that Wagner plants his leit-motifs in *Tristan*. Proust's use of the word "overture" is more than merely a literary convention. It is the choice of a deliberate method. We are being introduced to one of the grand operas of literature, one in which musical construction—the announcement, development, and repetition of themes—plays as important a part as the action.

There is a third "way," but we will not know it until we reach the very end of *The Past Recaptured*, the last volume of the novel. It is the way of art and it is slowly built up in Proust's re-creation of the work of three characters who represent it: Vinteuil, the composer, Bergotte, the novelist, and Elstir, the painter. (There are other artists in Proust, like the actresses, Rachel and Berma; Octave, a rich, young nonentity at Balbec who turns out later to be a talented theatre designer; Dechambre, the pianist; and Morel, the violinist. They are none of them creative artists in the same sense as Vinteuil, Bergotte, and Elstir, though they exemplify Proust's notions about art in various ways. Berma, particularly, is important because Marcel learns from her that great acting consists in the suppression of personality, not its exploitation. Morel has a far more complex role in the novel than that of being a violinist, though there is never any doubt that he is a superb one.) It is our narrator Marcel, however, who shows us the process by which the enchantments of love and society become disenchantments, and are then transformed into art.

There is another dualism in *Remembrance of Things Past*. In *The Past Recaptured*, Marcel makes the following comment in regard to his plan for the book he is about to write:

> Soon I was able to show a few sketches. No one understood a word. Even those who were favorable to my conception of the truths which I intended later to carve within the temple congratulated me on having discovered them with a microscope when I had, on the con-

trary, used a telescope to perceive things which, it is true, were very small but situated far off and each of them a world in itself. Whereas I had sought great laws, they called me one who grubs for petty details. (PR 393–394)

There is, in this statement, an uncharacteristic defensiveness. In truth, Proust reaches for "great laws" through "petty details," and he uses, figuratively, both the microscope and the telescope as instruments of perception.

The microscope and the telescope share in common lenses of magnification. The first deals with the invisibly small; the second with the invisibly distant. As such, the first is an instrument of space, the second an instrument of space-time. When we look at an amoeba under a microscope, what is minute is merely enlarged. We assume that process can be stopped in order to be described. When we look at a star through a telescope, an abstract system of geometry must be brought into play in order to make what we see have meaning, for the star is at a distance that has become transformed into time—time no longer measurable in terms of human consciousness, such as minutes and years, but only in "light years," an abstract concept of the mind that does not proceed from the senses. Empirical description in the microscope is transformed, in the telescope, into conjectural analysis. In the first, we observe phenomena; in the second, we try to understand the laws that govern them.

Proust offers for our inspection slide after slide under a microscope. Just when we think we have looked most closely, he reminds us that what we are looking at is, if not false, certainly partial. We have forgotten about time, which is altering the specimen under the lens as relentlessly as it is altering the observer. Our eyes glued to the aperture, we barely notice that a telescope has been substituted for the microscope.

Like the substance of space-time through which we look up at the stars, the forgotten years that lie behind, or the unsuspected years that stretch ahead of any moment effect the quality of that moment though the perceiver may not be aware of it when it is occurring. Process cannot be arrested, except in death. Even then, it continues in physical decomposition, and because the dead are still able to provoke changes in the living. Proust attempts to do two things at once: to arrest the moment; and to show us the moment hurrying on to qualify itself, to contradict itself, even to nullify itself. No fact or phenomenon is too minute for Proust to examine thoroughly; yet each of these examinations is placed in a structure so vast, seen from a viewpoint so timeless that what at first appears to be a worm's-eye view of reality turns out, in the end, to be a dazzling reach of perspective. Like the effect of the "zoom" lens of a camera, we start infinitely close to the object and find the field of vision increasing in depth, distance, and meaning. The microscope-telescope figure is uniquely relative, for no matter how large the small may be made to appear, it remains, always, in ratio to distance.

In Proust, we have two analogical metaphors that have application to the microscope and the telescope. The magic lantern of his boyhood is similar to the microscope. It enlarges the image it projects. Windows are analogous to the telescope. Though no physical magnification takes place, the significance of what is seen by a particular viewer is calibrated in exact ratio to the psychological distance of the viewer from the scene. The lesbian seduction scene between Mlle. Vinteuil and her anonymous friend that Marcel sees in the window at Montjouvain has a special meaning for him. That meaning becomes apparent only if we draw a triangle connecting it to a scene that precedes it in time and another that follows it. The past scene is the Combray bedroom scene in which his mother withholds her good-night kiss. The future scene is that one when, on the train back from La Raspelière to Balbec, Albertine innocently lets Marcel know, for the first time, that Mlle. Vinteuil's lesbian friend is also an intimate of hers "who has been a mother, a sister to me, with whom I spent the happiest years of my life at Trieste, and whom for that matter I am expecting to join in a few weeks at Cherbourg, when we shall start on our travels together . . . and I know Vinteuil's daughter almost as well as I know her. . . ." (CP II 361–362) (It is of interest that Albertine's statement, which revives past experiences for Marcel and is a premonition of those of the future, should in itself contain both a past and a future threat: ". . . with whom I spent . . ." and "whom . . . I am expecting to join. . . .") In the imaginary triangle connecting these three scenes—the Combray bedroom, the Montjouvain window, and the train between La Raspelière and Balbec—each corner of the triangle depends on the others.

Marcel's reaction to Albertine's statement is too intense; after having decided to give her up, he does an about-face and decides to marry her. It is at that moment we realize there is something wrong with our narrator. He is more than just a nervous and sensitive young man. He is emotionally disabled. His decision makes it necessary to re-examine the true meaning of both the Combray bedroom scene and the Montjouvain scene, whose significance becomes apparent, retrospectively, in the anguish Albertine's statement causes him. And the import of both scenes will shift again when we learn that it is Mlle. Vinteuil's nameless friend who is responsible for rescuing Vinteuil's septet from oblivion. The Montjouvain scene has further consequences but it will suffice for the moment to point out that what at first was merely descriptive now demands interpretation; "petty details" require the application of "general laws." The emotional lives of Marcel and Albertine distinguish them as individuals, but the general laws that govern emotional lives transform them into general types. Albertine's lesbian history has the power to harm Marcel precisely because lesbianism is not singular. Marcel's capacity for suffering is the result of his particular emotional make-up and is also a *form* of suffering we have already seen illustrated in Swann's obsessive jealousy of Odette.

Like the stars, which seem stationary and whose courses are relative to the speed of the earth's revolutions and its position in the universe, Proust's characters are transfixed by the moment and stirred by its relation to past and future moments. The relativity of time adds a dimension to personality as it does to physics. Proust illustrates this by a series of jarring revelations as carefully adjusted as a time bomb—in a seven-volume edition of Proust, it takes Marcel three volumes to discover that Charlus is a Guermantes, and one more to find out he is a homosexual. Revelation in Proust is intensified by the length of time we are made to wait for it, and its power, though it appears to increase through difference, actually increases through similarity. What *appears* to be different becomes the same, once the specimen has been stained by time. The clarity of the lens, the keenness of the vision behind it, are trifles by comparison. Personality is by nature incongruous, being a product of time. Time, at any given moment, tends to obscure this. Taken as a whole in any given lifetime, it reveals it. After the Princesse de Guermantes' death, Bloch mistakes Mme. Verdurin—the new Princesse de Guermantes—for the old one. It is a perfectly understandable mistake *at* the time but not *in* time. As readers, who have followed the process of her evolution, we know very well that Princesse de Guermantes who was once alive and is now dead. To us, Mme. Verdurin is still Mme. Verdurin.

Proust uses two other methods to demonstrate the relativity of time to perception: direct statements about it, and indirect shifts in the structure of the novel itself. There is one telling example that combines both and occurs at that moment when, having told the story of Swann and Odette's love affair—which took place before he was born—and before he picks the story up again in chronological time, the narrator suddenly switches to the present. An old man, now (and we had been deluded into thinking he was a child!), he goes back to the Bois de Boulogne to recapture the days when he would linger there to catch a glimpse of Odette:

> The reality that I had known no longer existed. It sufficed that Mme. Swann did not appear, in the same attire and at the same moment, for the whole avenue to be altered. The places that we have known belong only to the little world of space on which we map them for our own convenience. None of them was ever more than a thin slice, held between the contiguous impressions that composed our life at that time; remembrance of a particular form is but regret for a particular moment; and houses, roads, avenues are as fugitive, alas, as the years. (SW 611)

If there is a duality in the viewpoint of the novel (Marcel, the observer; Marcel, the observed), in its structure (the two "ways"), and in its theme (the problem of a reality equally perceptible in the opposed dimensions of the microscope and the telescope, the present and the eternal), there is also a duality in its subject in plain terms of human consciousness. And that is the important distinction Proust makes between "the name" and "the place"—or, more appropriately, "the thing," for the distinction bears, finally, upon everything. In the Proustian universe, nothing is what it first appears to be: there is a prevision that attaches itself to the mere names of places, people, and events. This early vision is preverbal—not involved with the word per se but the sound of the word.

To a child, names are magical sounds that precede and then identify objects of reality. These must, of necessity, be in the immediate vicinity: familial figures, domestic objects, personal effects. (This childhood fascination with sound is repeated when Marcel is an adult in his description of the cries of the street hawkers of Paris, the names of the railway stops on the "little crawler" that connects Balbec with Douville, and his interest in the etymology of place names and titles.) The magic of a sounded word identifying an object is in direct proportion to the distance of the object, for, imagination intervening, the object may be shaped to the sound in any number of fantastic ways. Thus, though it is his mother's kiss Marcel excruciatingly needs, the sound of the word "Swann" has more magic than the word "mother." Swann is at a further remove. Fantasy, conjecture, and reverie are fed by the partially known, the barely glimpsed, the overheard. Need, physical and direct, is too painful to be magical, and carries no sound. Desire, mental and distant, admits of any possibility. Venice and Parma sound all depths. Françoise is in the kitchen.

The sense of place is never disinterested. Wherever one is seems permanently fixed; wherever one is not is invested with glamour. Both notions are illusory. The sense of place merely precedes the sense of dislocation. The security of Combray produces the romance of Balbec, the boredom of Balbec the excitement of Venice. Susceptibility is the key to interest.

Before Marcel sees Balbec, he imagines it as a stormy, northern coast of mist and cold, on the edge of which a church built in the Persian style is perched. This notion comes to him from Swann, who acts, for Marcel, as a kind of sinister travel agent, imbuing foreign places with the fantasies of nostalgia rather than the limitations of fact. When Marcel arrives at Balbec, he makes a pilgrimage to the church before he gets to the town proper, and finds it in a square as pedestrian as the one at Combray. A sign across the street reads "Billiards." Balbec itself is a bustling seaside resort with a grand hotel. Actuality contends with the haunted coastline of the imagination, the exotic image of the Persian church.

Obstructed by a vision he created out of the sound of words, Marcel misses also something of the reality before him. In a typical Proustian twist, Elstir, in a later scene, explaining the carvings of the Balbec church to Marcel, confirms the presence of a Persian sculpture that Marcel failed to see:

> Some parts of it are quite oriental; one of the capitals re-
> produces so exactly a Persian subject that you cannot ac-
> count for it by the persistence of oriental traditions. The
> carver must have copied some casket brought from the
> East by explorers. (WBG II 196)

Place, then, is one of the first instigators of expec-
tation and, therefore, one of the cornerstones of dis-
enchantment. It is merely one link in a chain of similar circumstances. Marcel's notion of what Berma's
performance of *Phèdre* will be like is utterly different
from what he sees. Around the billboard announcing the presentation of the play, Marcel constructs his
own performance. The real thing disappoints him; it
takes him years to discover the true nature of Berma's
genius. Similarly, the railway timetable is, in *Swann's
Way*, "the most intoxicating romance in the lover's library." (SW 421) By the time we get to the second volume of *Cities of the Plain*, Marcel can say "in the timetable itself, I could have consulted the page headed:
Balbec to Douville via Doncières with the same happy
tranquility as a directory of addresses." (CP II 356)

Near the end of *Remembrance of Things Past*, Mme.
Sazerat, a Combray neighbor, turns up at the Venice
hotel where Marcel and his mother are staying. At a
table in the dining room, Mme. de Villeparisis and
Norpois, the diplomat, who have been lovers for years,
are having lunch. During Mme. Sazerat's girlhood,

her father had ruined himself for Mme. de Villeparisis'
sake. Anxious to see this beautiful creature on whose
behalf her family had suffered so much, she asks Marcel to point out Mme. de Villeparisis, whom she has
never seen. What she now sees is an old, dried-up,
little woman whose face is marred by a hideous ec-
zema. She does not believe this person is Mme. de
Villeparisis; she can only imagine Mme. de Villeparisis as permanently young, eternally beautiful, forever
capable of inducing pain. Mme. de Villeparisis, "the
thing," and Mme. de Villeparisis, "the name," have become separated.

But there is still another turn of the screw. Emotions may make illusions of perception. Time can
make illusions of the emotions. If the old Mme. de
Villeparisis has never been real to Mme. Sazerat, who
can only imagine her in a perpetual present, so Mme.
de Villeparisis, the young heartbreaker of the past, has
never been real to Marcel either. Seeing Mme. Sazerat's illusion, he understands his own. They are both
taken in by "the name," even if their misconceptions
come from opposite directions in time. Though there
are as many realities as there are perceivers, one quality of reality can always be taken for granted: it cannot be truly perceived at any point in time without a
knowledge of the past *and* the future. Points of time
are artificial and deceptive; they foster the illusion that
they are real and complete in themselves.

Proust attempts to get at reality from three points of
view at once, the past, the present, and the future. The

structure of his book cannot by intention be chronological. It is, rather, centrifugal. The floating narrator, trying to fall asleep, slowly becoming aware of the various rooms and places in which he has lived, might be compared to a spider at the center of a circular web, spinning a world out of his own consciousness. The web, already finished in his own mind, allows him to dart to this point or that on the rim of the circle—flying away from the center, then back. His book expands successively outward and downward from himself. Or, like a pebble thrown in a pond, each incident in Proust widens out to its farthest perimeter.

The enchantments of the past must always become the disenchantments of the future. But memory, a preservative, may intervene. The embalmer of original enchantments, it is the only human faculty that can outwit the advance of chronological time. Art, the embalmer of memory, is the only human vocation in which the time regained by memory can be permanently fixed.

It is these two saving graces that Proust enshrines in a world that has no others.

II

THE GARDENS

---

*I had already drawn from the visible stratagems
of flowers a conclusion that bore upon a whole
unconscious element of literary work . . .* (CP I 4)

If, like a botanist, one were to search through *Remembrance of Things Past* for flowers, one would be surprised at the size of the bouquet. Swann's way is a country of lilac and hawthorn; hawthorn, particularly, is to be the flower that reminds Marcel of Combray. Its pink exquisite version is found on the way to Swann's house, and it is also a religious flower, whose white species not only decorates the church of Saint-Hilaire at Combray during festivals but "arranged upon the altar itself, inseparable from the mysteries in whose celebration it was playing a part, it thrust in among the tapers and sacred vessels its rows of branches." (SW 158) The Guermantes way is strewn with water lilies and violets. These flower images are not merely decorative. For the opening action of *Swann's Way* takes place in a garden, and around that garden the rest of the novel gradually crystallizes, each memory lighting up a bit of space here, a piece of time there in the narrator's fluid consciousness, until all its elements are solidified. This seemingly random process is actually rigidly circumscribed. As each of the characters, places, and themes appear, adding shape to the novel's structure, and density to its coloration, the architectural mass of the novel accumulates power. Its form is mysteriously unknown to us at first; each fine stratum added to another builds up, finally, to solid rock. It is difficult sometimes to make out the shape of the rock; it is hidden by flowers whose forms are evocative and whose scents are overpowering.

Just as the madeleine dipped in tea—a tiny garden image in itself, for the tea consists of lime blossoms steeped in water—is the magic potion from which all of Combray is to be released, so Aunt Léonie's garden, so real originally, becomes that ideal ground, the perpetual springtime of childhood.

We have three gardens to begin with: the one attached to Aunt Léonie's house; the hawthorn and lilac along the Méséglise way; and the water lilies and violets that perfume the Vivonne along the Guermantes way. About each of these gardens, the three "families" cluster: Marcel's, Swann's, and the Guermantes'. They are all Combray, and around that magic land, that garden from which a child is expelled—in the same way that Adam was expelled from the garden of Eden, and for much the same reason—a universe begins to expand, as magical in its embodiment as the genie escaping from the bottle.

Tiny as Aunt Léonie's garden is, it includes a Gethsemane. Swann's ringing of the garden gate bell—a sound which is to re-echo throughout all of *Remembrance of Things Past*—carries the sound of doom to Marcel. It means he will be sent to bed early; his mother will forego his good-night kiss, that kiss upon which all his security and well-being depend. Marcel tries to force his mother to kiss him good night by sending her a note through Françoise, Aunt Léonie's faithful servant and cook. When there is no response to this, he waits, trembling, at a turning of the stairs to intercept her. Her negative response—she is, after all, interested in "curing" him of his neurotic dependency—is surprisingly countermanded by Marcel's father, who sees that Marcel is suffering and suggests that Marcel's mother spend the night in his bedroom. Marcel falls asleep while his mother reads to him from George Sand's novel, *François le champi*.

This forcing of the issue, this "involuntary" kiss seals Marcel's fate. An emotional "fix," it is the negative of a photograph that will be developed many times. In ridding himself of one anxiety, Marcel inherits others. Through this submission on his mother's part, Marcel unconsciously learns that suffering is a way of being loved, that love, once freely given, can be demanded. By being willful, he has, paradoxically, been *allowed* to suffer a paralysis of the will. One other important thing should be noted: though it is his mother's love Marcel needs, it is through the power of a man, his father, that he is permitted to receive it. Watching Swann, his mother, and his father in the garden through his window, waiting for his mother to relieve him of his agony, he becomes a spy, the watcher whose beloved object is kept under surveillance until what he must irrationally possess becomes his. The full flowering of the implications of this incident is elaborated in his love for Albertine, five volumes later, but here, at the very beginning, we have all the precipitating influences that will determine Marcel's emotional life. Since there is no security in a possession based on anxiety, the act must be repeated over and over again. Love is not a choice but a desperate reassurance, and the greatest power such a love has is the cessation of anxiety. The repetition of this ritual is the psychological key to the character of Marcel, in which suffering and love are inextricably bound. (Marcel's grandmother, though she also wants to "cure" him of his dependency, does not have the power to withhold a ritual token essential to his happiness. There is, also, no third figure behind his grandmother with whom Marcel can compete. Because of this lack of compulsion, it is his grandmother, rather than his mother, who represents genuine love throughout the novel.)

From this early event, the night Marcel's mother spends in his room, we move backward and forward in time through a series of "gardens"—landscapes and seascapes—each of which is to be a place of suffering. The romance of Swann and Odette is pieced together by Marcel through the conversation and memories of other people. The relationship of Swann and Odette is the nourishing soil from which the emblematic tree of Marcel's life is to spring. Each furthers various romantic illusions that are to influence Marcel's life deeply. Through Odette, he is subtly connected in his youth with the themes of love and art. There are three incompatible "portraits" of Odette. Marcel first meets her as a boy at his Uncle Adolphe's house in Paris where she is known to him simply as "the lady in pink." He is aware that she is a courtesan though he hardly knows what the term implies. He knows she is "bad" and interesting, yet she seems so like everyone else, except for her air of luxury and refinement, the stylishness of her clothes. Later, when he sees Elstir's portrait of her as "Miss Sacripant," in which she is dressed as a man, he is disturbed by her again, partly because he knows her without quite recognizing her, partly because of the transvestite nature of the portrait itself. Between these two portraits, another intervenes: Swann's comparison of Odette to the "Zipporah" of Botticelli.

Odette has, from the beginning, the excitement of the forbidden, a suggestion of evil, particularly since what makes her so is invisible to Marcel as a child, and becomes attached to the figure of Gilberte during his boyhood. Gradually joining Odette's circle, one of the young men who pays court to her image rather than to herself, Marcel is caught up in the complication of her roles: the "fast" woman of Combray, the courtesan he meets at Uncle Adolphe's, Swann's wife in Paris, and the mother of Gilberte. Odette is a distillation of both the biological and social strands of the novel. She is the personification of a sexual secret, and she is fashionable. Proust creates a bouquet around her by associating her in a thousand ways with flowers: her winter garden, her chrysanthemums, her violets, her orchids. A courtesan's life is lived in privacy—a privacy whose greatest compensation is luxury, and, to Odette, flowers are both luxuries and symbols of the luxurious. In a marvelous expansion of metaphor, Proust merges these various facets of Odette into a general observation on the relationship between flowers, trees, and women:

> I had heard that Mme. Swann walked almost every day along the Allée des Acacias, round the big lake, and in the Allée de la Reine Marguerite. I would guide Françoise in the direction of the Bois de Boulogne. It was to me like one of those zoological gardens in which one sees assembled together a variety of flora . . . this, the Bois . . . was the Garden of Woman; and like the myrtle-alley in the Aeneid, planted for their delight with trees of one kind only, the Allée des Acacias was thronged with the famous Beauties of the day. (SW 597)

> . . . from a long way off . . . long before I reached the acacia-alley, their fragrance, scattered abroad, would make me feel that I was approaching the incomparable presence of a vegetable personality, strong and tender; then, as I drew near, the sight of their topmost branches, their

lightly tossing foliage, in its easy grace, its coquettish outline, its delicate fabric, over which hundreds of flowers were laid, like winged and throbbing colonies of precious insects. . . . (SW 598)

In Odette's house, after her marriage to Swann, "There was always beside her chair an immense bowl of crystal filled to the brim with Parma violets or with long white daisy-petals scattered upon the water. . . ." (WBG I 237) In the passage quoted above, there is one reference to water, "the big lake," and, interestingly enough, in a scene that connects two important gardens together, we get the same brief juxtaposition of the floral and the marine. It is the scene in the Champs-Elysées where Marcel wrestles with Gilberte. He saw her first in Swann's garden at Tansonville, where she beckoned to him from a distance by sketching "in the air an indelicate gesture," one he assumes is a deliberate insult, but which, for him, has a definite sexual connotation. In the second garden, the Champs-Elysées, we come upon this passage:

I held her gripped between my legs like a young tree which I was trying to climb; and, in the middle of my gymnastics, when I was already out of breath with the muscular exercise and the heat of the game, I felt, as it were a few drops of sweat wrung from me by the effort, my pleasure express itself in a form which I could not even pause for a moment to analyse. . . . Perhaps she was dimly conscious that my game had had another object than that which I had avowed, but too dimly to have been able to see that I had attained it. (WBG I 193)

It is immediately after this scene, that Marcel has an involuntary memory. The moldy smell of the urinal in the Champs-Elysées reminds him of his Uncle Adolphe's room at Combray. The linking of flowers and water—the Champs-Elysées and the water closet—of the later garden and the early one should not be lost on us, for it is through Uncle Adolphe that Marcel first met Odette, and it is Odette who makes possible, both biologically and socially, Marcel's relationship to Gilberte.

The floral images of *Swann's Way* are superseded by the marine images of *Within a Budding Grove*, and both kinds of images thread themselves through the remainder of the novel. Elstir's paintings are a clue to this. Françoise's asparagus, which Marcel describes in detail at Combray, turn up in *The Guermantes Way* in a painting of Elstir's called "Bundle of Asparagus," and in his painting of the harbor at Carquethuit, the land images—of the town, the church, the promontory—are painted in watery colors and forms, whereas the sea is depicted as if it were on land. The plain of Swann's way, the river of the Guermantes way are, slowly, being joined.

Water lilies float on the surface of the Vivonne along the Guermantes way. It is a water pipe at the Princesse de Guermantes' that restores to Marcel a moment in the "marine dining room" at Balbec. A bowl of water, a lake, a few drops of moisture, and a urinal connect the Champs-Elysées with the Combray of Adolphe, Odette, and Gilberte. They connect further with the underground bathing establishment at Balbec that Albertine used to frequent. It is there, after her death, that Marcel sends Aimé, the head-waiter of the hotel, to investigate Albertine's lesbian connections. It would not be too farfetched to say that they prefigure Marcel's trip with his mother to Venice. Proust connects everything with fine wire, and just as Swann and Odette use the word "Cattleya"—an orchid—as a code word for sexual intercourse, so it is to be another and rare orchid that waits to be fertilized by a bee in the Duchesse de Guermantes' courtyard in that remarkable scene in which Charlus and Jupien meet, and, performing a ritual as predeter-mined as any in the instinctual world of biology, rec-ognize each other as homosexual partners.

These images open out even further. Not only is the dining room at Balbec "marine," but so are the dining room and garden at Rivebelle. And if a performance at the Opéra is transformed into a subaqueous theatre of the Nereids, so an aquarium is the very metaphor Proust uses as a description of Charlus' way of living:

> And so M. de Charlus lived in a state of deception like the fish that thinks that the water in which it is swim-ming extends beyond the glass wall of its aquarium which mirrors it, while it does not see close beside it . . . the shadow of the human visitor who is amusing itself watching its movements, or the all-powerful keeper who, at the unforeseen and fatal moment . . . will extract it without compunction from the place in which it was happily living to cast it into another. (CP II 268–269)

Balbec itself is a "water garden"; on one side, it faces the sea; on the other the countryside where Mme. Verdurin's estate, La Raspelière, is located, as well as the Cambremer's estate, Féterne.

The garden deities move toward the water, and Marcel's mother, a major one, is transferred from a garden to a seascape near the end of the novel when she and Marcel finally take the trip to Venice. By then, we have been through every female relationship of Marcel's life. The figure of the mother outlasts them all. When we reach Venice, we have moved more than the great distance that separates the flowers and streams of Combray from the world's only city of water. We have moved backward in time to that fateful moment when the seed is planted in the soil. A Gothic window overlooking the Grand Canal faces the same sort of view Marcel saw from the window of Aunt Léonie's bedroom.

Swann is a kind of unwitting Mephistopheles to Marcel's Faust. Through Swann, Marcel falls in love with the illusion of place, the idea of love, and the vocation of art. Swann is more than Marcel's mentor, however. The very name of Swann is a magic essence:

> The name, which had for me become almost mythological, of Swann—when I talked with my family, I would grow sick with longing to hear them utter it; I dared not pronounce it myself, but I would draw them into the discussion of matters which led naturally to Gilberte and her family. . . . All the singular seductions which I

had stored up in the sound of that word Swann, I found
again as soon as it was uttered. (SW 206–207)

Proust planned originally to divide *Remembrance of
Things Past* into three parts: the *Age of Names*, the *Age
of Words*, and the *Age of Things*. The preverbal magic of
the name Swann, like the bell that sounds to announce
his arrival, attaches itself to the Swann that is a world
in himself as well as to the worlds Swann discloses to
Marcel. This bewitched sensation repeats itself in the
name "Guermantes," and casts its spell on such notions
as travel, love, and social position. It is the necessary
luster through which Marcel apprehends the surface of
reality. Swann is enchantment's personification, and,
as such, a blinder of vision in person; every delusion of
Marcel's life is threaded through the figure of Swann.
There are three special reasons for this:

1) Swann is, in himself, a cause of Marcel's pain,
being the immediate though unknowing catalyst of
Marcel's agony on the night his mother withholds her
good-night kiss.

2) Causing pain, Swann nevertheless has experienced its equivalent in his relationship to Odette.

3) Marcel follows Swann's example throughout
life, repeating the major experiences Swann undergoes, but transcends the limitations of Swann's life by
discovering the secret of time regained and by committing himself to the vocation of art.

Swann is the pilgrim without knowledge watched
over by the enlightened proselyte who has outdis-

tanced him. Swann is Marcel, the nonwriter; Marcel, the writer, is Swann transfigured. Swann acts as an example, frozen in the world of love and society, who glimpses the faintest lights of the world of illumination and hears the distant echoes of a world escaped from time. Like Marcel in the bedroom scene, Swann's will is the index of his weakness. He acts, but against himself. Having come to see the emptiness of life, he sees nothing else. Swann's great curse is that he is not an artist; he is a connoisseur of art. He is damned in the same way that a nonbeliever might be in a religious book who is always a hair's breadth away from revelation and dies having missed the secret of redemption. He is sympathetic, but he is our study in error. Nevertheless, he leads a saint into the wilderness—and by furnishing a bad example, out of it—and near the very end of *The Past Recaptured*, the last volume of the novel, Marcel states clearly the influence of Swann on his life:

> But if it had not been for Swann, I would not even have known the Guermantes, since my grandmother would not then have renewed her acquaintance with Mme. de Villeparisis and I would not have met Saint-Loup and M. de Charlus, which led to my meeting the Duchesse de Guermantes and, through her, her cousin, so that it was also through Swann that I happened at this moment to be in the house of the Prince de Guermantes, where the idea of the book I was to write had just come to me suddenly—which meant that I should be indebted to Swann, not only for its subject but also for the decision to

undertake it. A rather slender stem, perhaps, to support
in this way the entire expanse of my life! (PR 247–248)

Each of Marcel's loves—Gilberte, Oriane de Guermantes, Albertine—belongs to special landscapes.
Gilberte travels from Swann's garden at Tansonville
to the Champs-Elysées; the Duchesse de Guermantes from a legendary countryside filled with castles
and feudal demigods to her mansion in Paris with its
garden courtyard where a rare plant waits for a bee
to fertilize it; and Albertine from the seaside at Balbec to imprisonment in Paris. Each of these flowers
seemingly so firmly fixed in its original soil rises up
from its roots and spreads its tendrils in various directions. To know Gilberte, Marcel pursues the Swanns.
As he becomes an intimate of Odette's drawing room,
a friend of Swann's, he moves further away from his
original object, Gilberte. Starting out to be a lover, he
ends up a family friend.

And Albertine is, from the beginning, part of a
"little band." Marcel falls in love with a group of girls
at once—*les jeunes filles en fleur.* Capable of causing him
the deepest anguish, Albertine is finally singled out.
She, even more than Gilberte, is insubstantial. Gilberte is various but less diffused. There is the Gilberte
who goes to tea parties, the Gilberte who is Swann's
daughter, the Gilberte who plays "prisoner's base" in
the Champs-Elysées. (It is interesting to note this
game, for, later, Albertine is to be referred to as "the
prisoner.") In Albertine, Marcel attaches himself to an

enigma, compounded of sea and sky—("Albertine preserved, inseparably attached to her, all my impressions of a series of seascapes . . . I felt that it was possible for me on the girl's two cheeks, to kiss the whole of the beach at Balbec.") (GW II 73)—and yet tantalizingly human, an enigma impossible of solution, for it would be just as easy to say that Albertine becomes attached to the enigma of Marcel. Albertine is cunning and devious, but in a kind of endless reflection of facing mirrors, it is impossible to tell where Marcel's version of her ends and her own begins. With Gilberte, Marcel preserves her original image by detaching himself from her. With Albertine, he plunges into a sea that has no discernible depth. So convoluted, so sensitized does his love for Albertine become, that, in a kind of reverse recoil, she seems to ape the object she sees reproduced in his eyes. Albertine moves in a bourgeois world, conventional on the surface, intangible in reality, and filled with perverse glimmerings—a world of middle-class girls disporting themselves at the beach, disappearing into the countryside, playing "ferret," which, like Gilberte's game of "prisoner's base," Marcel is finally allowed to join. But what he joins is not an ordinary group of girls but a tangle of ambiguous goddesses, slipping in and out of each other's identities—the mobile consciousnesses of the sea and the sky, which nevertheless exude the strong flavor of vegetation:

As on a plant whose flowers open at different seasons, I had seen, expressed in the form of old ladies, on this Bal-

bec shore, those shrivelled seed-pods, those flabby tubers
which my friends would one day be. (WBG II 267)

Through the Duchesse, the mysterious world of
the Guermantes, so absolutely impenetrable to Marcel,
he thinks, gradually becomes accessible. What is revealed is not the magic of ancient names and distinctions, but human failure, duplicity, and vanity. These
three women are all shimmer and mystery when Marcel first meets them; they are processed, in time, by
reality, but a reality in itself questionable, for the perceiver changes at the same time as the objects that undergo a metamorphosis beneath his gaze.

These three loves, though they are all failures, differ from each other in important ways. Marcel gives
Gilberte up as if the suffering his love for her entails
is too much to bear. He protects that love by refusing to allow it to be nurtured toward a conclusion; he
draws back to avoid further pain. Haunted by doubt,
doubt becomes obsessive. It is only late in life that he
realizes that Gilberte was attainable. She confesses
she was attracted to him, at the very end of the novel.
At the time their relationship takes place, he with-
draws in order to sanctify the image of his love rather
than risk its failure. In this retreat, we have a narcis-
sistic, almost masturbatory version of love. The picture, or image of the beloved, is more precious than
its actual presence—just as the lantern slides of Geneviève de Brabant are always to be the ideal against
which the Duchesse de Guermantes is to be mea-

sured. So the idealization of women—like places—is always fatally inconsistent with knowing them. Like the two ways, where geography becomes mental, so, here, physicality and personality become internalized. The true Gilberte exists inside Marcel, not outside him. Marcel destroys and preserves his relationship to her at the same time. Oblivion accompanies separation. But by not coming to any issue, the relationship forms an unconscious pattern for those of the future, as it reinforces the emotional patterns of his behavior toward women that began with his mother. If love can be deliberately demanded, it also can be deliberately killed.

Mme. de Guermantes inspires love by awe; her name is evocative, magical. She is not a person who turns into an illusion like Gilberte, or an illusion that turns into a person like Albertine. She is inhuman to begin with. Proust says that the love for a person is always the love of something else as well, and, in the Duchesse, Marcel becomes obsessed with the power of the feudal overlord who is still a member of the contemporary world—a world so select, so special, that, to Marcel, it might as well be the Middle Ages. If, with Gilberte, he falls in love with the legend of Swann, with the Duchesse, he falls in love with the history of France. It is not her wit, her style, her position, or her beauty that ultimately matter; it is that in her name she embodies a history; in her face and person a race; in her speech a landscape and an epoch; and in her manners a civilization. Though her intelligence, her modishness, her *ton* impress everyone as they do herself, to Marcel, after he has sifted the real jewels from the fake, it is another quality that counts: her conservativeness, in the real sense, for here, in person, is the prototype of something worthy of conservation. The Duchesse, the greatest lady of her day, and Françoise, the servant, share qualities in common. Their speech and their manners are feudal; the serf and the lord possess virtues enhanced by the existence of each other. The farmer and the landowner, still bearing the fragrance of the soil, enrich each other's powers. In *Remembrance of Things Past*, Françoise and the Duchesse have no reason to meet. Yet they have more in common than either could possibly imagine. They are two terms that have become separated in one of Proust's metaphors.

In the social world of the day, the Duchesse is something else again: she is powerful because of who she is, and more powerful because she knows how to exploit herself. Mme. de Guermantes lives a life Marcel can only imagine; since that is his chief way of perceiving life in general, she becomes a wheel within a wheel. A great lady smiles at him in church at Combray; he follows her through the streets of Paris; and imagines the ghost of her haunting the snow-hushed streets of the army town of Doncières.

What he is searching for is the enigma of history, the charm of the person exempt from humanity. As the Duchesse becomes human, she loses her charm and history its enigma. (In the same way, diplomacy becomes dull in Norpois, medicine absurd in Cottard.) Marcel spies on the Duchesse waiting along the route he knows she is to pass. As he did with his mother, with Gilberte, he *watches* her. By the time he knows whom he is watching, he is watching somebody else.

Albertine is the great love of Marcel's life, and in Proust's description and analysis of their relationship, we have the most original, hypnotic, and accurate dissection of obsessive love in fiction. Proust's portrait of Albertine is a final accomplishment in a theory of personality implicit throughout the book. People do not only become different *in* time; they are different from time to time: the observer undergoes analogous changes. Proust's characters seem to be attending a long costume party, in which one disguise is doffed after another, but their costumer is changing clothes at the same time. At the last great party given at the Princesse de Guermantes (the former Mme. Verdurin), he describes the decline and old age of his characters as if time had dressed them in various disguises. In truth, they were in disguise always; each revelation in Proust occurs from a slightly different angle. It is the process of character that defines it; since character is only made manifest in time, there is no other definition. Even a minor character like Legrandin illustrates this, for when we first meet him, he attacks snobbery violently. We meet him later and discover he *is* a snob; in fact, he is haunted by snobbery. And when we see him finally, after he has entered the Faubourg Saint-Germain through the marriage of his nephew, he is no

longer interested in it, or going out to parties. The rev-
olution has come full circle; the infatuation of a lifetime has wasted itself on nothing. If we can conceive
of Legrandin being observed by viewers other than
Marcel at various times in his life, we can see how
many versions of Legrandin could be made up.

All these inconsistencies, all these turns of the
screw, become consistent in the end. Realism in fiction never corresponds to reality in life, because it pre-
supposes an impossible point of view—that one which
lacks a viewer. A reality is always real to *some*body.
As soon as it is, the viewer must be included with the
view. Proust argues against realism effectively and provides the ultimate demonstration. Proust is the most
honest of novelists because he shows us not only how
little we know about other people but how impossible it is to know them. It is a suspicion we have always
had but hate to see confirmed. The confirmation does
not warm us; nevertheless, we cannot deny it. Proust,
like the genius psychologist he is, makes the inconsistencies take on a consistency of their own, just as
Chekhov, in the theatre, shows us how the seemingly
irrelevant lies at the heart of relevance. The patch-
ing together of what appear to be opposing traits performs a function similar to that of a metaphor, for only
those actions that are dissimilar but capable of connection can create a whole character out of superfi-
cially irreconcilable kinds of behavior. The power of
metaphor is not merely descriptive but psychological;
the link between two things we were not aware of is

revealed to us. Farfetched it may be, even bizarre; we know instantly, though, whether it rings true. When it is successful, it has two virtues: it increases our sense of credibility by refusing to win us over easily, and it sharpens our sense of revelation. Mme. Verdurin's anti-Semitism and her Dreyfusism would seem incompatible. Once we understand that she is a professional cause-monger who needs only a cause célèbre and can switch from Dreyfus to Debussy without a qualm, the inconsistency vanishes. It has helped, nevertheless, to make Mme. Verdurin real.

Charlus moves through *Remembrance of Things Past* like a mobile statue constantly being resculpted. The revisions have no effect on verisimilitude. Only once, in Proust, in the revelation of Saint-Loup's homosexuality, is this sure grasp of the basic nature of personality questionable. Proust "springs" it on us; we don't quite believe it. What we feel is his obsession to reveal rather than the truth of the revelation.

In this sense of character as metaphor, Albertine is Proust's consummate creation.

Who is Albertine? She is the unknowable animal who calls forth the finest resources of Marcel's intellect. The greatest analytical mind in the world is helpless confronted with a dog. It is Marcel's fate to want to see what cannot be seen: the sex life of a plant, the emotional histories of the deep-sea creatures, the motivations of the dark. Marcel and Albertine are two liars hopelessly tangled together. She charms him by being out of the range of what analysis can reach. To keep her in focus for a further try, lured by what he cannot know, he falls in love with her.

Albertine is Marcel's sensibility turned inside out and objectified. The greater pretense in their relationship comes from Marcel. Her reserve in the face of his jealousy, her lies, her restlessness all prod him on to another attack. *If* he knew, he keeps saying, he would be happy. But it is precisely because he doesn't know that he loves her. A scientist in a dressing gown, he watches over a laboratory of falsehoods, the greatest one being that he is objective in regard to the truth. Marcel uses Albertine to keep from himself a truth about himself: he is not in love with Albertine, he is in love with what Albertine loves.

As such, he credits her with a power and a reality she doesn't have. Albertine is addicted to games—particularly "diabolo"—clothes, cars, ice cream, planes. She is far simpler than he and far more deceptive. His lies are lies of the mind, hers of being. In Albertine, Marcel is matched against himself in a battle that cannot be finished. She holds within herself the two sexes in one and is, therefore, a constant reenactment in her very existence of the ideal torture of the voyeur. Albertine is the window scene of Montjouvain, the courtyard scene of Charlus and Jupien played over forever and ever.

It is no wonder that her commonest attributes, her polo cap, her mackintosh, the way she plays the pianola, her stride along the front—every physical manifestation of herself—take on an Olympian sheen. Marcel grasps at every vestige of her reality because he has made her up the way the Greeks made up their gods: he needs constantly to be reassured that she is *there.* Albertine is both a deity in Proust's "Garden of Woman" and the demon at the center of his vision, for he describes her as "a mighty Goddess of Time" under whose pressure he is compelled to discover the past. Starting out with the mystery of the animal, she ends up with the mysteries of eternity.

There is another important female deity at Combray, the owner of the house herself, Aunt Léonie. Like Marcel, she is a perpetual watcher, a hypochondriac confined to her bed, nursed on two equally powerful illusions: the illusion of her illness, and the illusion of its cure. Marcel inherits more from her than even he is at first aware of. Love becomes for Marcel a similar phenomenon, and, characteristically, takes on the symbolic form of illness. Like Aunt Léonie, Marcel develops an incurable disease, asthma. Suffocated by the scents of the flowers that he loves, he is forbidden the garden forever.

THE WINDOWS

My curiosity emboldening me by degrees, I went down to the ground-floor window, which also stood open with its shutters ajar. (CP I 2)

While Marcel waits for his mother to come up and kiss him good night, he peers down into the garden through his bedroom window. That window is to become a point of view, a transparency more viable than that which ordinarily separates the spectator from the visible while it makes vision possible. In Proust, the window is, psychologically, the voyeur's picture. Accidental images of other people's pleasure fulfill a painful need in the viewer. Contributing a power within himself to what he sees, Marcel is the victim of what is to be seen.

We are introduced to the window device in a subtle way. In Marcel's room at Combray, he looks at the lantern slides of Golo and Geneviève de Brabant, that ancestress of the Duchesse de Guermantes who first stirs the sediment that is to coalesce around the Duchesse's name and person. Marcel is able, by manipulating the projector, to focus the magic lantern slides on any part of his room. Their images are both deeded and willed.

There is a finespun association between the colors of the lantern slides and the colors Proust uses in the scene in which Marcel first sees the Duchesse in church. In the slides, Geneviève de Brabant wears a blue girdle, the castle and the moor are yellow, and the body of Golo, overcoming material obstacles, floats on the walls, on the door handle, wearing his red cloak. His face is described as pale. Here, in part, is the church scene:

> Suddenly, during the nuptial mass, the beadle, by moving to one side, enabled me to see, sitting in a chapel, a lady with fair hair and a large nose, piercing blue eyes, a billowy scarf of mauve silk, glossy and new and brilliant, and a little spot at the corner of her nose. And because the surface of her face, which was red . . . (SW 250)

This passage is followed by this interesting connecting link to the lantern slides:

> . . . we were uncertain, till then, whether we were not looking merely at a projection of limelight from a lantern . . . (SW 251)

And ends thus:

> Her eyes waxed blue as a periwinkle flower, wholly beyond my reach, yet dedicated by her to me; and the sun,

bursting out again from behind a threatening cloud and
darting the full force of its rays on to the Square and into
the sacristy, shed a geranium glow over the red carpet laid
down for the wedding, along which Mme. de Guermantes smilingly advanced, and covered its woolen texture
with a nap of rosy velvet, a bloom of light. . . (SW 255)

The colors of the lantern slides and the stained-
glass windows, both illuminating figures pertinent
to the Duchesse's genealogy—Gilbert le Mauvais in
stained glass, Geneviève de Brabant in the lantern's
hues—shine down and through the Duchesse de
Guermantes. They suggest, too, the fluidity of the apparently stable, the immateriality of what appears to
be real. Just as Golo and Geneviève de Brabant can be
focused on a doorknob in Marcel's room, so the light
of the Duchesse's stained-glass ancestors focus their
past illuminations on her, transcending her physical
body, making her—as Marcel sees her—something
more than mortal. The affinity between the lantern
slides and the stained-glass windows is one of the finer
shades on Proust's palette, for it is to be through the
"lenses" of windows that Marcel is to observe certain secrets of life, each one enlightening a mysterious
past he did not understand, or projecting a significant
image into the future.

At Montjouvain, on one of Marcel's solitary walks
along the Méséglise way, he falls asleep outside Vinteuil's house. When he wakes, he sees the first horror
scene of *Remembrance of Things Past*, Mlle. Vinteuil's
seduction by a woman friend, preceded by the sadistic

ritual of spitting on Vinteuil's photograph. This scene follows one in which Marcel yearns to seduce a peasant girl—one who will be an extension of the countryside itself, a female avatar of the local ground, a precursor to the spectral landscapes locked up in the bodies of Gilberte, the Duchesse, and Albertine. What is the point of this scene?

A serious relation between sex and art is being established, for it is through his love for his daughter, and the misery her lesbian attachment causes him, that Vinteuil, a country tunesmith—our first impression of him—is transformed into a great composer. And it will be, ironically, this very same friend of his daughter's who will save Vinteuil's septet for posterity by meticulously collating various manuscripts of the score that Vinteuil left behind him when he died. Like Aunt Léonie's delusions, this woman is both a "cause" and a "cure"; ruining Vinteuil's life, she redeems herself by preserving his art, part of whose greatness is attributable to her very existence. It is also the first introduction of the homosexual theme in *Remembrance of Things Past*. Significantly, it will be through a window again that Marcel sees the meeting of Charlus and Jupien, their recognition and ritual pattern of seduction. This second revelation sheds a further light on the meaning of the first.

These two scenes—Montjouvain and the courtyard scene that opens *Cities of the Plain*—are linked in many fashions, aside from being two explicit visions of sexual perversion. The pollenization of a rare orchid by a bee, the only insect that can fertilize it, picks up the biological motif with its flower metaphor, a motif implicit in the earlier scene in Marcel's desire to possess a human fragment of the Méséglise soil. Both scenes are seen through windows, and both scenes require the presence of a passive viewer whose existence is unknown to the participants. To Marcel, the helpless witness of both, they are more than prurient visions; they are *happenings* that are to have the profoundest effect on the future of his life.

Homosexuals play a particular biological role in *Remembrance of Things Past*. Acting behind windows through which their secrets can be observed—windows that often overlook gardens—they illustrate both the irrationality of human emotions and the capriciousness of nature. Like the rare orchid that waits to be fertilized by a bee in the Duchesse de Guermantes' courtyard, Charlus and Jupien exemplify a rare form of existence. Created from, but not creating life, they are a form, nevertheless, that has existed always. If instinct has become insidious in Swann's choice of Odette and Marcel's of Albertine—choices that go counter to probability and reason—Charlus' choice of Morel goes counter to biology itself, if one assumes the purpose of biology to be reproduction. The impossibility of homosexual relationships in Proust is vitiated by two facts: the pervasive maternal fog through which he sees *all* sexual relations, and the lack of a noncompulsive heterosexual relationship that might form a standard of comparison. If love itself is a disease psychic in origin, but as predictable in its ultimate effects as pneumonia or cholera, it matters little how diseased any particular version of it is. In Proust, the homosexuals are just as unhappy as the heterosexuals.

Homosexuals cannot be distinguished by any biological peculiarities observable to the scientist. They cannot necessarily be detected socially by any overt behavior. Being secret, they represent the qualities of secrecy. To the heterosexual made aware of their existence, as Marcel is at Montjouvain and in the Duchesse's courtyard, the homosexual becomes a permanent reminder of the unconscious nature of sexuality per se, of the irrationality and power of all sexual attraction.

Convincing as Proust may be, there is one peculiarly illogical drawback to the biological and psychological function homosexuals serve in his novel: Chosen as exceptions to illustrate a general theory of love, the more they illustrate it the less exceptional they become.

In society, homosexuals form a tenacious underground. At the Princesse de Guermantes' party in *Cities of the Plain*, the usher announcing the Duc de Chattellerault has slept with him a few days earlier, under the impression he was an "Englishman." A footman, unaware of Charlus' identity, offers to introduce him to the Prince de Guermantes, a relative to whom Charlus hardly needs an introduction. And Charlus himself, one of the great arbiters of French society, a man who sets the tone for a whole civilization, winds up in a male brothel being beaten by a male prostitute.

(The inefficacy of the paid-for beating is not merely one irony gilding another, it is the final, rotted core of the disease of the ideal. Even here—chosen, arranged for, paid for, in a house Charlus has helped set up for just such an occasion—the experience is unsatisfactory. The prostitute, a good sort, is not able convincingly to simulate hostility.) The freemasonry of homosexuality is a red thread binding the beggar to the king, the ambassador to the footman. The secrecy of the homosexual, the hypocrisy of society are twin mirrors. Each must pretend something; disguise is the necessary catalyst to both.

Homosexuals, a society within a society, are rooted in a biological incongruity, perpetually subject to social judgment, just as society, in a larger sense, springs from a false conception of human relationships, and is perpetually at the mercy of individual criticism. The mysteries of genetics produce a secret sect; the arbitrariness of genealogy (and, later, money, for the Duchesse de Guermantes' "breeding" is no more fortuitous than Mme. Verdurin's "millions") produces its social equivalent—the world of the Faubourg Saint-Germain.

A minority group, driven by guilt and producing it, homosexuals are, according to Proust, outcasts of society only because society casts them out for its own special purposes: the survival of any social group depends on the ability to exclude. At the Verdurin musicale at Quai Conti, Charlus first excludes Mme. Verdurin, isolating her, through rudeness, from what he considers her social superiors. Then she excludes him by

turning Morel against him, who publicly denounces
Charlus. In each case, the weapons are social: status
and prejudice. It is the Queen of Naples who rescues
Charlus, taking him by the arm and leading him out
of the room. We are back where we started: the Queen
is putting Mme. Verdurin in her place.

Because the homosexual is forced to assume a false
social role, he is, paradoxically, a microcosm of society itself. The homosexual generates the condition
that precedes social grouping, exclusion; as a member
of society, he is a travesty, therefore, of its mechanics.
The social grouping of the homosexual is of particular
interest to Proust because only a single arbitrary area
of connection among individuals is necessary for the
formation of the group. Thus, in the Dreyfus case, the
social equivalent of this psychological process occurs.
The Faubourg Saint-German and the anti-Semitic
elements of the bourgeosie, ordinarily without any
interests in common, find themselves in a forced but
mutually profitable alliance. Similarly, it requires only
Swann's passion for Odette to make him fall in love
with the Verdurins—at first—when, in actuality, they
are the very sort of people he detests. Homosexuality
is most illustrative here because it produces the condition of least choice: psychological compulsion. Homosexuals cannot help excluding what they cannot in-
clude, heterosexual love. Society must pretend to be
equally helpless. The Duchesse chooses whom she is
to see in only a very limited sense; that is why it is
important both for her prestige and self-esteem to as-

sume an enormous range of possibilities: She will go to this party, but not that, receive this particular person, but not the other. Actually, like the homosexual, her choices are precircumscribed.

Charlus shares with Swann a distinction accorded only these two characters: they are observed, but they are also extensions of the observer: Swann is the heterosexual version of the Marcel who is observed, Charlus the homosexual one. They each occupy roughly similar positions, Swann dominating the first half of the book, Charlus the second. We infer this splitting up of character from the following facts:

Swann's love affair with Odette, though it occurs many years before Marcel's birth, is a similar relationship to that of Marcel and Albertine. In spite of the difference in time, both relationships revolve at their beginnings around the closed circle of the Verdurin "little clan" and both have Vinteuil's "theme" as their leit-motif. Vinteuil's sonata belongs to Swann, his septet to Marcel. More significantly, the psychological patterns are similar: it is the enigmatic nature of the woman, the torture of her absence rather than the pleasure of her presence, that constitutes the clue to passion. The emotional exchange occurs within the lover, not between the lover and the beloved. It is jealousy that primes the heart rather than mutual satisfaction. Swann's jealousy is felt most keenly at a point where he becomes aware of Odette's having had lesbian contacts as well as heterosexual ones—this fear of Odette's inversion becomes more credible if we connect Swann-Marcel with Odette-Albertine than it would be as an isolated fact. For there is nothing in the rest of Odette's life or Swann's history of jealousy to explain this rather unexpected phenomenon. By the time Swann marries Odette, he is no longer in love with her: she has freed him from jealousy, she who was both its object and its cure, and she has detached him from the social world of the Faubourg to which he had belonged. Only one Faubourg daydream remains: Swann's fantasy of having Odette and Gilberte received by the Duchesse de Guermantes (the Princesse de Laumes at the time of Swann's marriage) as part of her intimate circle, a daydream denied Swann all his life and accomplished only after his death. Jealousy of a more specific sort drives Marcel into the labyrinth of Albertine's personality—his suspicions of her lesbian tendencies. But when Marcel returns from that labyrinth, he does not return empty-handed; he has been forced to explore the labyrinth of himself, at the end of which is the book we are reading. Albertine, too, detaches Marcel from the social world—more completely than Odette does Swann, for Odette at least substitutes the society of the petty bourgeois for the Faubourg. Albertine, kept prisoner secretly, disguised as Marcel's cousin on the few occasions when they go out, absorbs all of Marcel, his will drained by obsession. For Marcel, all social life becomes meaningless.

In both cases, impossibility is the great propulsion to love. Odette is domesticated, Albertine imprisoned. Under surveillance, they do not give up their secrets.

Swann marries Odette in the relief of liberation; Marcel lives with Albertine in the despair of imprisonment. But Swann's liberation is only delusive. Swann
and Marcel follow the same path; Swann goes part
of the way but not all of the way toward the truth.
Swann fails by succeeding; he marries Odette. Marcel
succeeds by failing, he loses Albertine, and writes his
book. The fineness of Swann's mind, the delicacy of
his perceptions remain those of an extraordinary dilettante, but a dilettante all the same. Death strangles
him with cancer among the nonentities of his life, who
never have really loved him. Marcel trades life for the
secret of time regained, the triumph of art. He does
not create a dilettante's work, like the book on Vermeer that Swann never finishes—or live a life Vermeer
might have approved of, which is Swann's pathetic jus-
tification of his own life—but a work of art worthy of
Vermeer himself.

If Swann and Marcel are the victims of a form of
love that creates its objects out of itself, making a genuine union impossible, Charlus' relationship to Morel
exemplifies the same general proposition. Love is
completely symbolic; the lover is half of a metaphor
constantly searching for its relevant image. The metaphor is never completed because the relevant image is
always itself. In homosexuality, where both terms of
the metaphor are more nearly the same, where there
is an actual duplication in the physical bodies of the
lovers, this version of love is given its most credible
demonstration.

In Marcel's love for Albertine, we re-explore the development of Swann's love for Odette, then step over a boundary on the other side of which lies the country of Charlus and Morel. The exploration is deeper, the nuances finer, the depths more horrifying. But essentially Albertine seems to be in part Odette, in part Morel; Marcel in part Swann, in part Charlus.

If a window is a transparency necessary to the voyeur, the ability to project images is necessary to the masturbator. The fact that crucial sexual scenes are witnessed in Proust through windows takes us back to the magic lantern of Marcel's boyhood. Like the window, it is a lens; unlike the window, it is held in the hand, it projects images, and it is manipulable. The lantern slides shed further light once we realize that Geneviève de Brabant was falsely accused by Golo of committing adultery. Even these seemingly innocent childhood images contained a sexual secret. Proust includes a masturbation scene in which the images of a window, a flower, and a tower are used:

> Alas, it was in vain that I implored the dungeon-keep of Roussainville . . . when, from the top floor of our house at Combray, from the little room that smelt of orris-root, I had peered out and seen nothing but its tower, framed in the square of the half-opened window, while, with the heroic scruples of a traveller setting forth for unknown climes, or of a desperate wretch hesitating on the verge of self-destruction, faint with emotion, I explored, across

the bounds of my own experience, an untrodden path, which, I believed, might lead me to my death, even—until passion spent itself and left me shuddering among the sprays of flowering currant which, creeping in through the window, tumbled about my body. (SW 226)

The sexual meaning of the window is not confined to Marcel. When Swann goes to visit Odette during the early months of their courtship, he taps upon her window as a signal for her to come to the door to let him in. And, on two separate occasions when Swann suspects Odette of deceiving him with Forcheville, the window image is invoked. Odette asks Swann to mail some letters for her, one of which is addressed to Forchevile. Swann reads the letter through the envelope, and confirms the suspicion that Odette has betrayed him:

> For a time Swann stood still there, heartbroken, bewildered, and yet happy; gazing at this envelope which Odette had handed to him without a scruple, so absolute was her trust in his honour; through its transparent window there had been disclosed to him, with the secret history of an incident which he had despaired of ever being able to learn, a fragment of the life of Odette, seen as through a narrow, luminous incision, cut into its surface without her knowledge. Then his jealousy rejoiced at the discovery, as though that jealousy had had an independent existence, fiercely egotistical, gluttonous of everything that would feed its vitality, even at the expense of Swann himself. (SW 407)

Later, he tries to peer through Odette's window to substantiate his fears. It is the wrong window and he wakens two sleeping old gentlemen. If the picture Swann sees framed in the window is not charged with the sexual meaning he expected, or the sexual intensity of the two homosexual scenes witnessed by Marcel, the scene is at least unconsciously consistent, for what Swann sees, no matter how comic or ludicrous at the moment, are two people of the same sex.

The image of two people of the same sex, a relief to Swann, is to become a torture to Marcel. When Albertine's friendship with Mlle. Vinteuil's anonymous lesbian partner is revealed, the scene he had witnessed in his boyhood behind the window at Montjouvain is set in motion; the dormant, still picture becomes animated. It is Albertine's capacity to make Marcel suffer that defines the nature of his love, and it is her invisible lesbianism that forms the substance of the long, analytical inquisition their relationship is to become. It is maternalness that Marcel seeks in his mother, and it is girlhood he seeks in Albertine. (". . . my love for Albertine had been but a transitory form of my devotion to girlhood.") (SCG 314) The particular horror of Albertine for Marcel is that she is not only the chosen deity who springs to life out of a general desire, but that she is his very competitor in that desire. (". . . all my desires helped me to understand, to a certain degree, what hers had been . . .") (SCG 140) She betrays him not only as a lover but as a man, just as his mother betrayed him earlier, in a more complicated sense, not only as a child but as a son. It is the emotional relationship Marcel has with his mother *combined* with the homosexual content of the Montjouvain scene that gives Albertine her special power. What Marcel feels and sees as a child comes true to haunt him as a fact—a fact he wants and does not want to know, since his pleasure consists primarily in his ability to feel pain—a direct association with Charlus who is explicitly masochistic and needs, finally, to be beaten with chains to feel sexual pleasure. What does pain-pleasure consist in for Marcel? Helplessness—the watching of the performance of others, either childishly, as in the bedroom scene; sexually and literally, as in the two window scenes; or figuratively, as in his obsessive jealousy of Albertine.

Marcel looks in at Mme. Swann's winter garden through a window, and out of the dining-room window of the Balbec hotel at the sea—against whose blue he draws the first portrait of Saint-Loup, and out of whose depths the goddess, Albertine, is to rise. He stares out the corridor window of the Grand Hotel at the countryside whose distant greenery encloses La Raspelière, the Verdurins' estate, and those small, provincial towns where Albertine goes on her "sketching expeditions," which, in retrospect, become the stations of the cross on the itinerary of the sexual prowler. Through the windows of the restaurant of Rivebelle he sees an intoxicated reality; and it is through a window of Elstir's studio that he sees Albertine racing by.

Looking out of the window of Saint-Loup's room, he sees the reflected shape of a hill that is to color all his memories of his stay at Doncières. Window images proliferate in Proust and are dramatically pulled together by a final association of three windows.

The linking of the "mother" window at Combray, and the two "homosexual" windows—the one at Montjouvain, and the one overlooking the Duchesse's courtyard—provides a tension between two subjects, establishes a bond between two emotions that is reenforced again in a further association. In Venice, Marcel describes a particular window at the hotel:

> On the piazza, the shadow that would have been cast at Combray by the linen-draper's awning and the barber's pole, turned into the tiny blue flowers scattered at its feet upon the desert of sun-scorched tiles by the silhouette of a Renaissance façade, which is not to say that, when the sun was hot, we were not obliged, in Venice as at Combray, to pull down the blinds between ourselves and the Canal, but they hung behind the quatrefoils and foliage of gothic windows. Of this sort was the window in our hotel behind the pillars of which my mother sat waiting for me, gazing at the Canal with a patience which she should not have displayed in the old days at Combray, at that time when, reposing in myself hopes which had never been realized, she was unwilling to let me see how much she loved me. Nowadays she was well aware that an apparent coldness on her part would alter nothing, and the affection she lavished upon me was like those forbidden foods which are no longer withheld from inva-

lids, when it is certain that they are past recovery. To be sure, the humble details which gave an individuality to the window of my aunt Léonie's bedroom, seen from the Rue de l'Oiseau . . . the equivalent of all these things existed in this hotel in Venice . . . she [his mother] sent out to me, from the bottom of her heart, a love which stopped only where there was no longer any material substance to support it on the surface of her impassioned gaze which she brought as close to me as possible, which she tried to thrust forward to the advanced post of her lips, in a smile which seemed to be kissing me, in the framework and beneath the canopy of the more discreet smile of the arched window illuminated by the midday sun; for these reasons . . . ever since then, whenever I see a cast of that window in a museum, I feel the tears starting to my eyes, it is simply because the window says to me the thing that touches me more than anything else in the world: "I remember your mother so well." (SCG 287–289)

The correspondence between the Combray bedroom window and the window in Venice, both maternal shrines, is here made explicit.

In the ultimate horror scene of *Remembrance of Things Past*, a scene whose implications project backward through four transparencies—the Venetian window, the window overlooking the Duchesse de Guermantes' courtyard, the Montjouvain window, and the window of Marcel's bedroom at Combray—we come upon the following passage:

And I heard the cracking of a whip, probably made still more cutting with nails, for I heard cries of pain. Then I

noticed that this room had a small, round window opening on the hallway, over which they had neglected to
draw the curtain; tiptoeing in the darkness, I made my
way softly to this window and there, chained to a bed
like Prometheus to his rock, and being beaten by Mau-
rice with a cat-o'-nine-tails which was, as a matter of
fact, studded with nails, I saw before me M. de Charlus,
bleeding all over and covered with welts which showed
that this was not the first time the torture had taken
place. (PR 131)

The "ultimate horror scene" for specific reasons.
For, if, earlier "My Hell was all that Balbec . . ." (SCG
141), this further vision of Hell peculiarly transcends
the personal and fuses the sexual and social motifs of
the novel. During a blackout, Marcel has taken refuge
in a building that turns out to be a male brothel run
by Jupien and supported by Charlus. He is first made
aware in this scene of Saint-Loup's homosexuality—a
suspicion confirmed when Saint-Loup carelessly leaves
behind his *croix de guerre* at Jupien's. The brothel scene
is immediately followed by the bombing of Paris. The
Paradise of Aunt Léonie's garden has led, by inevita-
ble stages, to a vision of Hell that is, psychologically,
the product of inversion (the brothel), and, socially, the
coup de grâce of Europe's ruling classes (the bombing).
Stupidity, corruption, malevolence, selfishness, disease—they are combined in two acts of aggression: the
beating of Charlus, the end product of centuries of civilization, and the attempted destruction of Paris, the
historical and material center of the same civilization.

It is no accident that three out of the four major male representatives of the French aristocracy in Proust's novel—Prince Gilbert de Guermantes (who spends a night with Morel at a house of prostitution at Maineville), Saint-Loup, and Baron Charlus—are all depicted at one point or another as patrons of male prostitutes. The one male Guermantes who eludes this category, the Duc, substitutes for it a lifelong obsession with adultery.

In *The Captive*, at a moment of great anxiety, Marcel experiences the following:

> Suddenly, in the silence of the night, I was startled by a sound apparently insignificant which, however, filled me with terror, the sound of Albertine's window being violently opened. (C II 546)

The sound, apparently insignificant, is of the utmost importance. It signals the departure of Albertine—an action suspected, dismissed, then actual, like Marcel's vision of the Persian church at Balbec, which is oriental in imagination, prosaic in reality, and, then, partly Persian in fact. But between the opening of this window, when Albertine makes the preparations for her departure, and her actual escape, she and Marcel take a trip to Versailles. Hearing a sound they cannot at first identify, Albertine says, "Why . . . there is an aeroplane . . . high up in the sky . . ." (C II 551–552)

It is at the violent opening of a window in his own house that Marcel suffers in anticipation the departure of Albertine. Like the other windows, this one sets the scene for a future surprise; Albertine not only parts from Marcel, she departs from life itself. This image of a window being violently opened, which fills Marcel "with terror," is thematically linked to the earlier brothel scene. Each one—for Marcel and Albertine have quarreled about her relationship to Andrée—involves the rediscovery of inversion, a real or symbolic reference to the French aristocracy (Guermantes, *croix de guerre*, Versailles) and the presence of an aeroplane (the bombing of Paris, Albertine's remark about the plane "high in the sky").

Like the ringing of the garden gate bell—a sound heard both at the beginning and the end of Proust's novel—the bedroom window at Combray becomes a repetitive motif. It narrows into a "peephole" behind which a once unimagined, and now desired and detested action takes place, transforming the childhood pictures of legend and history projected by Marcel's magic lantern into a horrifying vision of sexual love.

THE PARTIES

> *For every death simplifies existence for others, relieves*
> *them of the need of scrupulously showing their*
> *gratitude or the obligation to pay calls.* (PR 323)

The two books whose titles crop up most frequently in Proust are the *Arabian Nights* and Saint-Simon's *Memoires* of court life under Louis XIV at Versailles. *Remembrance of Things Past* draws sustenance from opposite poles: a book of exotic tales (whose genie emerges from a magic lamp, as Combray emerges from a cup of tea), and a masterpiece of social documentation. In *Swann's Way* and *Within a Budding Grove*, we are in a world of emanation; in *The Guermantes Way*, the lenses turn outward. The claims of the world are being investigated.

Proust's portrait of society has charm, wit, and grace—the cornerstones of civilized intercourse. It is, like love, however, a Pandora's box. Below the lid, in place of jealousy, ambiguity, and deceit, there lurk equally powerful monsters ready to spring: snobbery, mendacity, and fatuity. It is remarkable that Proust, having reached so dour a view of society, could reconstruct its original allurements. We are led into the labyrinth, dazzled by the lights, the conversation, the flashing of jewels. At the end of the maze is a *cul-de-sac*: society is no more rewarding than the people who make it up.

Three social groups are investigated by Proust: the bourgeoisie, the aristocracy, and their servants. The bourgeoisie is divided into the provincial characters of Combray, and the *nouveau riche* of Paris: the Verdurin "clan"; the bureaucrats, like the Bontempses; and the up-and-coming adventurers, originally proletarian or middle-class, like Morel and Odette. The aristocracy are the nobility and royalty, who have no significant distinction for Proust's purposes. Servants are exemplified primarily by Françoise, but also by Céleste Albaret (Proust's servant in actual life whom he made a character in his novel, presumably to avoid the easy identification of her with Françoise), the Duc and Duchesse de Guermantes' butler; Charlus' footman; Marcel's family butler; and a group of anonymous "herd" characters such as porters, chambermaids, footmen, chauffeurs, gardeners, coachmen, and so on. Of all these characters, only Françoise is drawn in depth.

Parties are Proust's main device for exhibiting social behavior; they are set like lozenges in the midst of the adolescent reverie, psychological analysis, and metaphysical speculation that form the greater part of the book. Each one is a solid block of realistic and satirical observation, contrasting sharply in style with the "interior" Proust. Innumerable minor social occasions are scattered throughout *Remembrance of Things Past*, and eight major ones of considerable length. Two of these occur during Swann's courtship of Odette; the other six belong to the narrator. They take place in the following order:

Swann

A dinner at the Verdurins' (SW 361–382)

An evening party at Mme. de Saint-Euverte's (SW 463–507)

Marcel

An afternoon reception at Mme. de Villeparisis' (GW I 256–391)

A dinner at the Duchesse de Guermantes' (GW II 148–327)

An evening reception at the Princesse de Guermantes' (CP I 47–170)

A dinner party at La Raspelière (the Verdurins' country estate) (CP II 63–169)

A musicale at Quai Conti (the Verdurins' house in Paris) (C II 304–444)

An afternoon reception at the Princesse de Guermantes' (PR 177–402)

The non-Verdurin parties—they cannot quite be called the Guermantes parties, since Mme. de Saint-Euverte, the hostess of the first, does not belong to that illustrious family—ascend the social scale in a definite order: Saint-Euverte, de Villeparisis, the Duchesse de Guermantes, the Princesse de Guermantes. They indicate again that Marcel and Swann are two facets of a single character, for this progression has social significance within the structure of the novel, and the first party, at Madame de Saint-Euverte's, is attended by Swann, while the second, at Mme. de Villeparisis', is attended by Marcel.

At the last reception at the Princesse de Guermantes' that concludes the novel, the Princesse is none other than Mme. Verdurin, a persistent monkey who has climbed the social ladder rung by rung. The middle-class pretenders and the pretentious aristocrats, now hardly distinguishable from one another, join hands in a final, macabre dance.

Jealousy is the controlling emotion of love, snobbery of society. The character most free of the first emotion ironically makes possible Proust's exhaustive examination of the second. Marcel's grandmother, in a typical Proustian surprise, facilitates Marcel's career in society by introducing him to Mme. de Villeparisis at Balbec. Mme. de Villeparisis, in turn, introduces Marcel both to Saint-Loup and Charlus. Marcel's grandmother is involved in a further irony: though she unwittingly sets Marcel's feet on the wrong path, it is she from

whom Marcel derives those moral values by which society is ultimately to be judged. We have, once more,
the paradoxical notion of the "cause" and the "cure"
combined. In this case, they are not double traits of
a temperament but an irony of circumstance. Marcel's grandmother shows her lack of social pretension
by not reintroducing herself to Mme. de Villeparisis,
with whom she went to school as a girl. It is Mme. de
Villeparisis who seeks her out and makes the Guermantes "contagion" possible for Marcel.

Marcel's grandmother is the moral center of his
social vision. She is the single person in Proust's novel
who is capable of feeling human love and who does not
undergo a transformation of character in the course
of the book. She is the steady beacon in the wilderness. Neither ironic nor sentimental, she is the pivot of
the Good around which the demons, giants, and monsters are made to whirl. Marcel's mother differs from
her in a specific way; from our viewpoint, rather than
his, she is involved in the etiology of his illness. But
a great ambiguity clouds the issue. After the grandmother's death, Marcel's mother is meant to take on
her own mother's qualities; she carries her bag, wears
her muff, quotes from Madame de Sévigné, and her
love for Marcel becomes unqualified by therapeutic
motives. Marcel's mother is clearly herself until the
grandmother dies. Then, we have one of those Proustian transfigurations in mirrors. She becomes shadowy
in two ways: by an alternation in the nature of her
character and by a switch in her function in the whole

scheme of the novel. Earlier, she establishes the emotional precedent on which Marcel's later relationships are founded. The good-night kiss she withholds and then bestows is repeated in Marcel's affair with Albertine, who refuses to kiss Marcel at Balbec and more than willingly kisses him, to his surprise, in Paris. He spends a great deal of thought on the reasons for the possible change, and he has good reason, considering his past, to do so. Moreover, in Marcel's indecisiveness at departing from Venice, in which he allows his mother to go off alone, and then at the last minute joins her, we have a repetition of his obsessive doubt in regard to Albertine. Marcel's mother loses her unconsciously projected "Albertine side" somewhere in the middle of the novel and is changed into the nonsexually charged character of the grandmother. Marcel's mother is equivocal, radiating at one time the emotional impact of Albertine, at another the beneficent influence of the grandmother.

Marcel's grandmother values only individual distinction. Social classes pursue the vested interests of a stratified society, and hold a variety of misconceptions in regard to each other. Marcel's family thinks of Swann only as a country neighbor married to a "loose" woman so far beneath him that Marcel's mother, a kind person indeed, refuses to meet Odette. That Swann is a friend of the Prince of Wales and an intimate of the Guermantes carries no weight. It goes unrecognized, or, if it is acknowledged, is reduced to "social climbing." Combray's view of society is as rigid as a Hindu's. People are born in fixed stations which can be changed only by a "brilliant career" or a "'good' marriage." Swann seems to have no career and has made an abysmal marriage. He is, to Combray, a rich stockbroker's son forever.

Odette's idea of the fashionable world is one of "smart places" where the "smart set" gather. It is not unlike a more contemporary version of "café society." A mistaken version—to begin with, at least—it tends to become true not because of Odette's acumen but because of the stupidity of social distinctions in themselves. It is a naïve misapprehension of a sophisticated truth. When Odette starts her "salon," Bergotte is her one social inducement, and it is around him that the civil servants, upper-class bourgeois wives, and bureaucrats gather.

The greatest misconceptions of all are the notions the middle class and the aristocracy hold of each other. They are equally fantastic:

> Nine tenths of the men of the Faubourg Saint-Germain appear to the average man of the middle class simply as alcoholic wasters (which, individually, they not infrequently are) whom, therefore, no respectable person would dream of asking to dinner. The middle class fixes its standard, in this respect, too high, for the failings of these men would never prevent their being received with every mark of esteem in houses which it, the middle class, may never enter. And so sincerely do they believe that the middle class knows this that they effect a simplicity in speaking of their own affairs and a tone of dis-

paragement of their friends . . . which make the misunderstanding complete. . . .

> . . . the two worlds take as fantastic a view of one another
> as the inhabitants of a town situated at one end of Balbec
> Bay have of the town at the other end: from Rivebelle
> you can just see Marcouville l'Orgueilleuse; but even
> that is deceptive, for you imagine that you are seen from
> Marcouville, where, as a matter of fact, the splendours of
> Rivebelle are almost wholly invisible. (WBG I 395–396)

Neither world survives Proust's inspection. In discussing the middle-class world of the Blochs, he says:

> . . . if, in "society," people are judged by a standard
> (which is incidentally absurd) and according to false but
> fixed rules . . . in the subdivisions of middle class life, on
> the other hand, the dinners, the family parties all turn
> upon certain people who are pronounced good company,
> amusing, and who in "society" would not survive a sec-
> ond evening. Moreover, in such an environment where
> the artificial values of the aristocracy do not exist, their
> place is taken by distinctions even more stupid. (WBG
> II 96–97)

Social pretensions affect the aristocracy to the same
degree as the bourgeoisie, with one qualification, of
which Saint-Loup is the chief example: aristocrats are
not vitiated by the dread of being considered inferior
because the idea has never occurred to them. (By the
same token, when Marcel asks Charlus why Mme. de
Villeparisis, who is a Guermantes, occupies an infe-

rior position in society, Charlus misunderstands the question, and discusses her marriage to a man less noble than herself. He seems unaware of her "inferior" position in the sense Marcel means, which is best described by the word *démodé*. To Charlus, she is a Guermantes and his aunt. That is sufficient.)

On the other band, the variety and energy of middle-class types is more commendable than a kind of physical standardization of the aristocracy, who are almost invariably ugly, with the exception of the Guermantes. In discussing the "little band" of girls at Balbec, Marcel says:

> The shrewd old money-changers from whose loins these Dianas and these nymphs had sprung seemed to me to have been the greatest of statuaries. (WBG II 200)

Albertine's family is as proud of its last name "Simonet" being spelled with one "n" as a Montmorency might be of his title. Morel pledges Marcel never to divulge the fact that he is a valet's son. Mme. de Villeparisis secretly longs for Mme. Leroi to attend her receptions because Mme. Leroi "cuts" her. Gilberte de Saint-Loup is attracted to the Duchesse de Guermantes because the latter has, in the past, refused to receive her. The Duchesse, in reverse, admires, at the end, only the world of actresses. The daughter of Berma, the greatest actress of her time, wants only to use her mother's reputation to gain admission to the world of the Guermantes. Snobbery, like love, leads to universal confusion and disappointment.

If the kindness of individuals—and here we judge from the viewpoint of Marcel's grandmother—is the only true standard of behavior, neither Saint-Loup nor the Duchesse de Guermantes can pass muster. And, in their cases, particularly, a telling distinction is drawn between manners and morals. Saint-Loup, un-selfconsciously exhibiting the inherited grace of the nobility, is so considerate that he races across the top of a banquette in a crowded restaurant to put an overcoat over Marcel's shoulders to protect him from the cold. Both the impulse and the acrobatic agility with which the action is accomplished are "aristocratic." Yet, he denies Marcel a photograph of the Duchesse, the most precious thing in the world to Marcel at the time. Saint-Loup is kindness itself to Marcel's grandmother during her illness, yet he refuses to be introduced to Odette at Mme. de Villeparisis' and is hideously cruel to his own mother. Similarly, Mme. de Guermantes, whose grief at the death of Saint-Loup is one of the few genuine emotions of her life, declines to intervene for him during his lifetime to save him from going to Morocco, a task she might easily have performed because of her great friendship with General de Monserfeuil. She suddenly pretends to know the general only slightly; it is not immoral to interfere, it is too much trouble.

The social scenes, followed by others of a recognizable pattern, have the quality of theses superseded by antitheses. Parties are immediately contrasted with human crises that involve the fateful moments of individual lives. After the afternoon reception at Mme.

de Villeparisis', which ends with the hostess pretend-
ing to be asleep so as not to have to say goodbye to
Bloch—a Jew and a Dreyfusard invited only because
of his access to "theatre people" who might be useful at
a later reception—we have two instructive scenes. In
the first, right after the party, Charlus, walking down
the street with Marcel, abandons him for a drunken
cabman. Another little piece of camouflage conceal-
ing Charlus' sexual life is torn away. The second scene
takes place in the Champs-Elysées. Marcel's grandmother goes to the public toilet. This toilet is run by a
woman who calls herself a "Marquise" and who says to
the park keeper in reference to her clientele: "I choose
my customers. I don't let everyone into my little par-
lors as I call them." (GW I 426)

Marcel's grandmother, who has overheard the
"Marquise's" statement, makes the most pointed of all
the social observations in Proust:

> Could anything have been more typical of the Guer-
> mantes, or the Verdurins and their little circle? (GW I
> 427–428)

We are shocked less by her comparing the "Mar-
quisc" to the Guermantes than by the fact that she
makes no distinction between the Guermantes and
the Verdurins.

This moral contrast of social versus individual life
is repeated again in a minor key a few moments later,
when Marcel takes his grandmother, who has suffered
a stroke, to see Professor E., a famous doctor. The

doctor barely has time to examine her properly. He is in a hurry. He is dining, appropriately, with the Minister of Commerce.

The most definitive version of this repeated lesson occurs after the dinner at the Duchesse de Guermantes'. Swann pays a call on the Duc and Duchesse before they go on to a costume ball. Swann awkwardly reveals that he is suffering from cancer and has only a few months to live. The Duc and Duchesse, preoccupied with the costume ball, pretend Swann is exaggerating and, being in a hurry, bid him the platitudinous farewells of social convention. The Duc then discovers that the Duchesse is wearing black shoes with a red dress. The Duc goes back to the house and fetches the red shoes. Hurrying Swann away, the Duc finds time to satisfy a pecadillo of fashion. There is in this scene a failure of standards all round, for Swann, the most delicate of men, is here too blunt. The coarseness of the graveyard is on him—the forms are less meaningful than we thought. Self-interest on the one hand, and death on the other make a mockery of civilized behavior. The disorder of life is not counterbalanced by the standards of society but is merely reflected in them at another level. That level, disappointingly, lies not at a depth but on the surface.

What Proust has to say about society is not new but incomparable. His ability to dramatize, the reproduction of speech, attitude, and manner, and the accurate observation of every social appurtenance—clothes, rooms, jewels, monocles, beards, furniture—all have the authority of a master—a master mimic as well as observer. The maliciousness and wit of the Duchesse, the bad punning of Cottard, the foredoomed timidity of Saniette, the academic tiresomeness of Brichot, the migraines, dislocated jaw, and false teeth of Mme. Verdurin, the painted flowers above which Mme. de Villeparisis greets her guests—all of it is set down with the double felicity of a great portrait painter and a first-rate playwright. The bourgeoisie gobble up the aristocracy, a quick mastication; the aristocracy absorb the bourgeoisie, a long digestion. Proust's book has been described often enough as the decline and fall of Europe's pre-World War I aristocracy. More accurately, it describes that moment, socially speaking, when a blood transfusion follows a bloodletting. The middle class pumped energy and money into a distinguished corpse. It is Proust's task to pursue vulgarity and sham down the darkest drains. The aristocracy and middle class, so distinct to themselves, are brothers, finally, under the skin. Birth and money, equally powerful talismans, invariably seek each other. Brought to the marketplace, they are exchangeable.

Exact, comic, relentless, Proust's social satire has the deadly accuracy of Daumier and the vitality of Hogarth. Imperative to the scheme of his novel, fascinating as documentary in themselves, Proust's social exhibitions lead us to two great catastrophes that have their initial germinations in the groups of people we have been watching—the Dreyfus case and World War I. Society is, after all, social.

The Dreyfus case is peculiarly modern. Civil government was threatened by the army; anti-Semitism was used as a weapon of concealment. Not a mere matter of culpability in high places, it was the first great national scandal in which politics and society could no longer be divorced. France was torn in two; and though a genuine moral issue was involved, each fragment of the national body followed its own predisposed interests—of class, money, and power. Proust discusses it both as a political and a social event, and reveals not the fatuity of justice—a reality in the Dreyfus case, and one to which Proust was personally committed—but the fatuity of human conceptions of it.

A public display of self-interest, the Dreyfus case broke the power of the army, the aristocracy, and, to a lesser degree, the Church. It brought stupidity to a national pitch. Even those on the "right" side were capable, as always, of cravenness and irrationality. Proust understood well the connection between political power and social interest, and while his main attack is on the bigotry of the anti-Dreyfusards, he is contemptuous of the fanatic partisanship on both sides.

Two rival salons develop out of the Dreyfus case. Mme. Verdurin, a Dreyfusard, is temporarily out of the running, but surrounded by her faithful "clan," she reaps an ultimate social benefit from the case:

> Mme. Verdurin, by the bond of Dreyfusism, had attracted to her house certain writers of distinction who for the moment were of no advantage to her socially, be-

cause they were Dreyfusards. But political passions are like all the rest, they do not last. . . . It was thus that, at each political crisis, at each artistic revival, Mme. Verdurin had collected one by one, like a bird building its nest, the several items, useless for the moment, of what would one day be her Salon. The Dreyfus case had passed, Anatole France remained. (C II 318–319)

Odette, vaguely "Nationalist," was felt to hold "sound opinions." Married to a Jew—Swann's conversion mattered little in the Dreyfus case—she got credit for patriotism and disinterestedness:

Mme. Swann had won by this attitude the privilege of membership in several of the women's leagues that were beginning to be formed in anti-semitic society, and had succeeded in making friends with various members of the aristocracy. (GW I 346)

On opposite sides of the fence, Odette and Mme. Verdurin are still two sides of the same coin. Mme. Verdurin, for all her "liberalism," is a firm member of her social group: "[Odette] was only following the example of Mme. Verdurin, in whom a middle-class anti-semitism, latent hitherto, had awakened and grown to a positive fury." (GW I 6)

The scales are balanced: a temporary social mistake in strategy, the result of stupidity on the part of Mme. Verdurin, and a social success, fired in the crucible of a convenient political tragedy on the part of Odette.

The absurd depths to which passions descended at the time are illustrated in an exchange between the

Guermantes' butler, who is against Dreyfus, and Marcel's butler, who is for:

> Ours let it be understood that Dreyfus was guilty, the Guermantes' butler that he was innocent. This was done not to conceal their personal convictions, but from cunning, and in the keenness of their rivalry. Our butler, being uncertain whether the fresh trial would be ordered, wished beforehand, in the event of failure, to deprive the Duke's butler of the joy of seeing a just cause vanquished. The Duke's butler thought that, in the event of a refusal, ours would be more indignant at the detention on the Devil's Isle of an innocent man. (GW I 407–408)

The Dreyfus case, despite its wide ramifications, uncovers the idiocy of social pretension and the meanness of human motives. The Duchesse despises the whole affair; she is forced to meet women at patriotic salons to whom she would not have nodded before the case started. The Duc loses the presidency of the Jockey Club because his wife is not considered "anti-Dreyfusard" enough. He blames his nonelection on his association with Swann. Saint-Loup, a passionate but temporary Dreyfusard, is influenced by his relationship to Rachel, a Jewish actress. Losing interest in her, he loses interest in the case. The Prince de Guermantes, an anti-Semite, momentarily recovering the traditional standards of honor by which he was brought up, becomes a Dreyfusard in spite of his prejudices. In the end, he does not have the courage to back up his convictions. Mme. Sazerat, back at Combray, refuses to bow to Marcel's father because she thinks he is anti-Dreyfus. Though there is some truth in this, Mme. Sazerat is more smug than just. Swann and Bloch, both Jews, are pro-Dreyfus. The Duc feels that Swann has betrayed his class, that Jewishness triumphs over moral delicacy, when, in truth, the situation is the other way around. Snobbery, a more personal passion than justice, is the prism through which a shattering historical event is seen.

One great social axiom pervades Proust, the geometric progression of misconceptions. The same absurdities of misunderstanding, often fatal, occur between individuals, social groups, governments, and nations.

As the Duchesse de Guermantes surprises us by the depth of her grief at Saint-Loup's death, so the Verdurins are shown suddenly in a sympathetic light. There is in Proust always a resistance to the evident. Who knows what further fact will cancel out a conclusion? The Verdurins use Saniette, the paleographer, as a whipping boy, mocking him in front of the other members of the "clan," and, more cruelly, in front of strangers. Shy, lacking self-confidence, Saniette is the perfect dupe. After the musicale in which Charlus is humiliated by Mme. Verdurin and Morel, and rescued by the Queen of Naples, the Verdurins discover that Saniette is ill and bankrupt. Generously, they give him an allowance for the rest of his life and go to great lengths to conceal the fact that they are the donors. Dr. Cottard is the intermediary; the pretense is that

Saniette has been left a legacy in Princess Sherbatoff's will. Saniette never knows that his true benefactors are the Verdurins. There may be a touch of condescension in this, it may merely be a gesture of remorse; nevertheless, Mme. Verdurin, who has just ruined Charlus' life, is shown, immediately after, as capable of an act of kindness, and one that reflects no glory on her. We get a new glimpse into a character we thought motivated only by self-interest.

Proust's entire vision of social life is colored by an ambiguity more pervasive than the twists and turns of character. We are presented with princesses who turn into drabs; the desire, in the first place, for princesses to be more royal than perhaps is possible undercuts the point of the revelation. The disappointed have more reason than most to inflate what they originally desired, as long as they live by disappointment. Proust's satire, often wildly funny, is still grounded in a reluctant melancholy. Relinquishing the very myths by which he lives, anxious not to perpetrate others, he remains an instinctive mythmaker. Idealistic but truthful, he is caught in the crosscurrents of the irreconcilable. The difference between the intensity of an improbable desire and the intensity of its real frustration can outweigh the distinction between desire and fulfillment. What one wishes never turns out to be true. But, then, how true is what one wished? By constantly asking the question, Proust minimizes the force of his original statement. Proust may have asked more of society than society pretends to give.

And, if we look closely, we can see where this ambiguity originates. No matter how contemptible the bourgeosie and the aristocracy turn out to be, we cannot rid ourselves as readers of the impression they made upon us before we were meant to see through the falsity of the impression. The world of Combray has moral values in which the good, the kind, and the generous operate. Combray is not only a straitlaced little Jansenist enclave but a place where a sense of what is appropriately human and fitting also exists and sheds some light. Marcel's mother and grandmother, reared in a narrow dogma, are neither narrow nor dogmatic. It is impossible not to see their values reflected in part in the other Combray characters, and in the nature of the town's life itself.

The aristocracy, too, have virtues. Grace and manner cast a spell that is not quite broken when we are shown the nastiness of truths that underlie them. Proust is in the position of having done his task too well. Like Milton's *Paradise Lost*, in which Beelzebub is more interesting than God, Proust's bedazzlements outweigh his lucidity. We are meant, like the narrator, to be blinded by diaphanous veils and then see through them. We cannot quite brush them from our eyes, and we have reason to suspect that he cannot either. Seen retrospectively, *Swann's Way* and *Within a Budding Grove* were written after disillusionment had set in. Yet both volumes create worlds more powerful than those that follow them. Proust is an extraordinary satirist and a superb thinker; but he is, when all is said and done, the great master of emanation. In *Swann's Way* and *Within a Budding Grove*, his boyhood and his adolescence provide material particularly suited to his supreme gifts. There is no world Proust cannot command; it is these two worlds, nevertheless, that are inimitable.

Understanding Proust's ultimate argument, we do not quite accede to it. Marcel's original impressions of Saint-Loup and the Duchesse de Guermantes are more lasting than their decline into vice and banality.

The social scenes in Proust have a value in the scheme of the novel not intrinsic to themselves. Set in huge blocks, incidents and occasions that occupy a short time span—hours or a day—assume a spatial mass out of proportion to the chronicle in which they are embedded. They are, literally, time-stoppers. The presumably wasted time that Marcel spends at these social occasions has a triple effect.

First, they make us aware of time in a special way by confusing us as to duration and speed. Hundreds of pages go by at which the activities of one evening are described. On the other hand, we can never quite figure out how many years separate Marcel's withdrawal from society and his last reappearance in it at the party that concludes *The Past Recaptured*. How long does he spend at the sanatorium before he returns to Paris? We do not know. Yet the day that Albertine is brought back from the Trocadéro by Françoise, and the day of Charlus' disgrace at Mme. Verdurin's are the same one. In the English text, this day takes up 287 pages. The action of the novel, clocked to an insidious stopwatch, successfully divorces the reader from an habitual view of chronological time.

Secondly, we are forced to another conclusion. Could these times really be wasted since they form such a huge mass of the novel? If Marcel's decision to be an artist stems from a special awareness of the nature of time, the very time he wastes, as long as it is *in* his novel, cannot be truly wasted. We do not mind his not going home to write and staying a little longer at the Duchesse de Guermantes'. We know something he refrains from telling us: he has written the very scene we are reading.

Third, these two notions in combination lead us to a third. It is the paradoxical role of the artist to be nourished on what irritates and what destroys. Vinteuil's greatness is clearly defined by Proust as an outcome, in part, of his suffering. Social life may be boring, and describing one dinner party more valuable than attending another. But we cannot quite get past the fact that, without attending one, dinner parties would have no value whatsoever.

In short, if social life had not been disenchanting, Marcel might well have spent the rest of his life as a dandy and a snob, transfixed by the dream of worldly success. We are in the strange position of deploring those temptations that kept him from being a writer when those temptations are the very things he is writing about. The negative value of social life in a book whose main theme is a writer's search for his vocation becomes positive in its very depiction.

If homosexuals make a particular biological point in Proust, Jews perform the same service on a social scale, and one of Proust's most original observations is the parallel he draws between the psychological patterns of the homosexual and the social position of the Jews. Discussing homosexuals, Proust says:

> . . . their love . . . springs not from an ideal of beauty which they have chosen but from an incurable malady; like the Jews again (save some who will associate only with others of their race and have always on their lips ritual words and consecrated pleasantries), shunning one another, seeking out those who are most directly their opposite, who do not desire their company, pardoning their rebuffs, moved to ecstasy by their condescension . . . having finally been invested, by a persecution similar to that of Israel, with the physical and moral characteristics of a race, sometimes beautiful, often hideous . . . taking pleasure in recalling that Socrates was one of themselves, as the Israelites claim that Jesus was one of them, without reflecting that there were no abnormals when homosexuality was the norm, no antiChristians before Christ, that the disgrace alone makes the crime. . . . (CP I 22–23)

In Bloch and Charlus, we get collateral life histories. A middle-class Jew, garrulous, iconoclastic, and often gross, over a lifetime becomes civilized. The

rebel joins the forces against which he rebelled. Bloch
ends up a famous and rich man, at ease in the world.
Though he has made a cult of his dead father, he marries his daughter to a Catholic and is absorbed into the
upper reaches of society:

> . . . Discretion, in both word and deed, had come to him
> along with social standing and age, with a sort of social
> age, if one may use the term. It is true that Bloch had
> formerly been indiscreet, as well as incapable of kindli-
> ness or friendly counsel. But some difficulties and some
> qualities are not so much attached to this or that indi-
> vidual or to this or that moment of existence, considered
> from the social point of view. They are, as it were, exte-
> rior to the individual, who passed through their beam of
> light as through various pre-existent, general and inevi-
> table solstices. (PR 312)

Charlus, a homosexual aristocrat, descends the
scale in the opposite order. The greatest social lion of
his day, his pride and arrogance lead to his rebuff by
Mme. Verdurin at the concert he arranges for Morel
at her house. Broken by Morel's leaving him, later suffering a stroke, he turns into that saddest of all social
creatures, a former giant grateful for any attention.

Bloch's pompousness, Charlus' overweening pride,
even Morel's conscious and self-aggrandizing cupidity,
offset by other human qualities, are made understandable in the long run. Proust's view of society and the
people who play its game is one of the most damaging
on record. Yet, there are no contemptible characters in

Proust, not because he is compassionate but because he is honest. He is able to transform Charlus, the least promising of all candidates—a social snob, homosexual, dandy, a man capricious to the point of madness—into a hero of gigantic proportions who has been compared, on more than one occasion, to Falstaff. He is an outsized comic-tragic figure. Proust shows us every ugliness of Charlus'. But Charlus is redeemed not by virtue of his intelligence, which is immense, but by a simple quality: a good heart.

At the vast spectacles of social display in Proust, a benign spirit hovers over the tables, salons, and gardens. It is Marcel's grandmother, more merciless than Mme. Verdurin or the Duchesse de Guermantes could ever be, judging every social malice from the unassailable viewpoint of human love.

THE STEEPLES

. . . an hour is a vase . . . (PR 212)

One day, walking along the Guermantes way, the weather darkens, and Marcel and his parents are given a lift in the local doctor's carriage. Dr. Percepied, before returning to Combray, has to pay a call at Martinville-le-Sec. At a bend in the road, Marcel has a strange experience. The twin steeples of Martinville church, seen from the moving carriage jogging along the winding country roads, join with the steeples of a third church, that of Vieuxvicq, in the distance, and begin to perform a complicated dance on the horizon. The sun is setting; the steeples—changing aspects of color, position, and shape—bob up and down, jump forward and back, in complex relationships that fascinate the boy. He has the feeling that something more than he can penetrate or understand "lay behind that mobility, that luminosity, something they seemed at once to contain and conceal." (SW 258) Suddenly, the carriage draws up outside the church at Martinville. Marcel is astonished at the illusions of perspective that made the steeples seem so far away in space, so distant in time. He feels an extreme pleasure in having watched them. The doctor makes his visit and, when they start out again, Marcel, sitting next to the coachman, who is disinclined to talk, tries to recall his experience:

> I was obliged, in default of other society, to fall back on my own, and to attempt to recapture the vision of my steeples. And presently their outlines and their sun-lit surface, as though they had been a sort of rind, were stripped apart; a little of what they had concealed from me became apparent; an idea came into my mind which had not existed for me a moment earlier, framed itself in words in my head; and the pleasure with which the first sight of them, just now, had filled me was so much enhanced that, overpowered by a sort of intoxication, I could no longer think of anything but them. (SW 259)

Marcel writes a short essay on the visual phenomenon of the steeples, which he leaves in a hamper in the carriage:

> . . . at the moment when . . . I had finished writing it, I found such a sense of happiness, felt it had so entirely relieved my mind of the obsession of the steeples, and of the mystery which they concealed, that, as though I myself were a hen and had just laid an egg, I began to sing at the top of my voice. (SW 261)

Many years later, driving in another carriage, with Mme. de Villeparisis and his grandmother, in the outskirts of Balbec, he has a similarly peculiar experience. As they come through a wood toward Hudimesnil, a town not far from Balbec, Marcel "is overwhelmed with that profound happiness which I had not often felt since Combray; happiness analogous to that which had been given me by—among other things—the steeples of Martinville." (WBG II 20) This time, he is looking at three trees:

> I could see them plainly, but my mind felt they were concealing something which it had not grasped, as when things are placed out of our reach, so that our fingers, stretched out at arm's-length, can only touch for a moment their outer surface, and can take hold of nothing . . . I recognized that kind of pleasure which requires . . . a certain effort on the part of the mind . . . that pleasure, the object of which I could but dimly feel, that pleasure which I must create myself, I experienced only on rare occasions, but on each of these it seemed to me that the things which had happened in the interval were of but scant importance, and that in attaching myself to the reality of that pleasure alone I could at length begin to lead a new life . . . I sat there, thinking of nothing, then with my thoughts collected, compressed and strengthened I sprang farther forward in the direction of the trees, or rather in that inverse direction at the end of which I could see them growing within myself. I felt again behind them the same object, known to me and yet vague, which I could not bring nearer. (WBG II 20–21)

The three steeples and the three trees carry a double-weighted meaning. They each produce a happiness like those Marcel experiences when he has an involuntary memory. Yet, in the first case, he takes pleasure in the moving objects themselves and in the mystery they conceal: the steeples tell him that time and space may be different from his consciousness of them. They do not lead him back to any past experience. In the second case, though the trees remind him of something, he is unable to dredge up any specific memory. Both the steeples and the trees are tantalizing suggestions of essences sealed up in matter, essences whose meaning Marcel cannot quite discover. Moreover, the steeples and the trees are directly linked to Marcel's evolution as a writer. His great relief, after he sees the steeples, comes from writing a short descriptive essay. In describing the incident at Hudimesnil, he makes a revealing statement: "that pleasure, the object of which I could but dimly feel, that pleasure which I must create myself. . . ."

The surfaces of reality hold imprisoned something more real than themselves. The name, the word, the thing—none is sufficient.

A question formulates itself: By what process can the essences sealed up in matter be made to reveal themselves?

The body, struggling with the unfamiliar, builds its cave at the Balbec hotel. Out of the hostile angles, surfaces, and depths, the distraught figure wrests a room in which he can lie down and sleep. Next door, his guardian angel, his grandmother, is poised to hear his three knocks on the wall, ready to come to his aid. Sound is dangerous, vision phantasmagoric; the night is interminable. An insomniac in a spider web manipulates the threads until he is its comfortable victim. Their ends are attached to distant places, familiar figures, sacred images, dreams, notions. He threads the room about himself, spider and fly at once. The light is lifting. He can breathe at last. The room, once malignant, is growing benign. Habit is constructing its habitation.

Time destroys. Memory preserves. Habit dulls. But habit is paradoxical and performs a double duty. The Combray bedroom has a high ceiling; the hotel bedroom a low one. As Marcel battles against the habit of sleeping in a high-ceilinged bedroom, he is, at the same time, forming the habit of sleeping in a room with a low ceiling. Habit enables us to cling to the familiar, to the self we think we know with a persistence almost irresistible. An anodyne for the terror of the unknown, it effectively keeps us from knowing, and is fatal in itself. Habit is a fiction the organism requires to dim perception. It screens us from the world, and from the true world of the self. Habit—no matter how intense the suffering it causes—is the last thing the personality will give up. It is arming itself against danger. The weapons may be more painful to use than the pain they seek to deflect. No matter. Habit allows us to live—by which Proust means it allows us to exist while it simultaneously compels us to miss Life.

The personality that is nothing but a collection of habits has little claim to being called a personality at all. The Marcel who turns the bad nonhabit of a high ceiling into a good habit is still a creature tortured by a fear of experiencing the unknown. To avoid it, he changes not the low ceiling but *who he was*. What enables him to do so is *not remembering*. This process of forgetting saves him from having to change *who he is*.

Habit requires a basic condition, a repeated response to a repeated stimulus. In time, the response will occur even when the stimulus is inappropriate. Habit is a half-remembered metaphor in which one term has lost its original relevance to the other. The sound becomes the thing; Pavlov's dog salivated at the sound of a bell. Habit is the enemy of memory for a simple reason: the metaphor of habit prevents the metaphor of memory from functioning.

Why is memory a metaphor? Memory connects two things through some object or sensation by sensing a correspondence between them. How does it differ from habit? Habit disconnects the past stimulus from the present response. Memory seeks the connection. Everyone's memory, therefore, contains millions of unique metaphors not necessarily discernible or rational. The assumption is, however, that no matter how different the connections may be, human emotions are basically similar. The scene Marcel sees in the Montjouvain window may be a unique experience. Yet, the discovery of a startling sexual secret in childhood would be practically universal. Similarly, rain brings back to Marcel the scent of lilac. It would not be difficult to transpose that sensation into a thousand analogous ones.

Human emotions may be similar; people are not. The sad fact is that we all cannot remember the same things. Worse, we cannot remember what other people have forgotten. *Those* are their secrets. Memory, which allows us by analogy to understand one another, also keeps us apart. The individual sensibility, in which each person is wrapped, as if in a cocoon, lures us on with the illusion of transparency, the belief in similarity. Actually, it is opaque, and what lies behind it is unknowably different. The immaterial soul of Albertine rising in her sleep as Marcel watches over her body separates them conclusively. Love, the attempt to recapture the memory of another person, can never be wholly satisfactory. Physical possession, verbal communication—neither gets at the fundamental nature of experience. Marcel cannot know what Albertine remembers. Albertine does not know what she has forgotten. Like the steeples of Martinville, the trees at Hudimesnil, the physical envelope of Albertine obscures her essential essence. Behind the window of her eyes, as behind the window at Montjouvain, memory may be performing an unspeakable act. Marcel has only to close his own to know how much can be hidden.

Of the three kinds of memory, conscious, unconscious, and involuntary, only the latter is of supreme interest to Proust. In conscious memory, the mind searches for the relevant fact by an act of will. Unconscious memory is a repression of connections, usually painful, which the conscious mind cannot dredge up as relevant fact.

Involuntary memory is like unconscious memory with two differences: 1) What stimulates it is immured in objects that decant the original sensation by chance, and only if, luckily, we come across those objects again in later life. 2) It is not, like unconscious memory, an unearthing of the past, but a reliving of the past *as the present*.

We may relive constantly and unwillingly an unconscious memory in our actions and psychological attitudes. In involuntary memory, we actually grasp the past as the present, as if time had literally stopped. No effort of will can achieve this since we have no control over the chance reappearance of things. Unconscious memory predisposes us to repeat what we have experienced. Involuntary memory induces perception and is not a repetition but a revelation.

It is difficult to separate unconscious memory from involuntary memory, but sleep, a paradox, helps to suggest the distinction: it is both the slave of habit and the liberator of memory. It leads us to time regained but is not time regained itself, for dreams are still under some form of conscious control—they are symbolic rather than real enactments. They allow us to remember what habit would have us forget, but we are permitted to do so only under the conditions of disguise. In involuntary memory, disguise is done away with; *then* becomes *now* in reality, not symbolically.

But when we say "reality," we must qualify again. Though the process of involuntary memory makes time past time present, and is not disguised like a dream, reality itself is merely the outer shell of a suprareality that is hidden from us. Albertine's body, the steeples, and the trees are apprehended by Marcel's senses. But they are all outer envelopes enclosing vital cryptograms to which he does not have the code.

Involuntary memory, unlike unconscious memory, is miraculous. It is here that Proust parts with Freud and moves out of the world of psychology into the realm of metaphysics.

We truly remember only what we have forgotten. Memory is a human form of time. It is all we know of it, and when memory ceases, in the insane, in the dead, we may assume that time ceases for those particular organisms. Memory is, even more than habit, supremely paradoxical. Being a form of time, it, too, is both a "cause" and a "cure"; eliminating every link between the scenes it portrays to us, it spares us the nonentities of our selves by allowing us to recollect the selves we were; but since we are able only to recollect the past, it hurries us on to our dissolution.

The true power of involuntary memory lies not in *what* we remember but in the process of memory itself. It restores to us not only experiences of the past but the selves that experienced them.

Hearing Vinteuil's "little phrase," Swann rediscovers a happiness he thought lost to him forever. To Swann, the "little phrase" has emotional content. Losses are partly regained in romantic nostalgia. Marcel, describing Vinteuil's septet, discovers something quite different. Relinquishing content, music is heard as pure form, the aesthetic equivalent of the temporal process. Eschewing every association, Vinteuil's music becomes not an inducer of memory but memory itself. We have, in Proust, the original concept of memory as a metaphor of time, not content; because of this, music is memory's most pertinent analogy. Form is apprehended as sensation; what is being formed is time. Marcel's involuntary memories satisfy a necessary condition: the common quality of being felt simultaneously at the actual moment and at a distance in time. This quality is the exact condition music demands of the listener; time connections make sound intelligible without any reference to the objective world.

We contain within ourselves every lost moment of our lives. It is necessary to be made aware that they are lost before we can regain them. Music informs us of this loss without specifying the nature of what we have relinquished. Like time, it tells us everything and nothing.

Involuntary memories are forms of ecstasy, "mne-monic resurrections" that do not contain earlier experiences so much as new truths. Sensations of the past are not duplications but sensation itself. Destroying the material world temporarily, they put in its place a world of revelation akin to the spiritual experiences of mystics, dissolving matter so thoroughly that

> ... if the present scene had not been immediately vic-torious, I believe I should have fainted; for, during the instant that they last, these resurrections of the past are so complete that they do not merely oblige our eyes to become oblivious to the room before them ...; they also force our nostrils to inhale the air of places which are, however, far remote; constrain our will to choose between the various plans they lay before us; compel our entire being to believe itself surrounded by them, or at least to vacillate between them and the present scenes ...
>
> Thus it was that what the being three and even four times revived within me had just enjoyed was perhaps, it is true, fragments of existence removed outside the realm of time, but this contemplation, although part of eternity, was transitory. (PR 200–201)

There are eighteen occasions in *Remembrance of Things Past* when Marcel has a memory—or an experience analogous to memory—significant enough to record. These occur in the following sequence:

1) The madeleine dipped in tea restores Combray in its entirety. (SW 61–66)

2) The steeples of Martinville suggest a hidden reality. (SW 257–261)

3) The moldy smell of the water closet in the Champs-Elysées reminds Marcel of his Uncle Adolphe's room at Combray. (WBG I 93)

4) The three trees at Hudimesnil awaken a memory Marcel cannot identify. (WBG II 20–23)

5) Flowerless hawthorns at Balbec bring back his childhood. (WBG II 309)

6) A steam heater recently installed in Marcel's bedroom hiccoughs while he is thinking of Doncières and, forever after, the sound is bound up with, or provokes memories of Doncières. (GW II 51)

7) Unbuttoning his boots, the living reality of his grandmother is restored to Marcel long after her death. (CP I 217–227)

8) Twigs burning in his bedroom fireplace recall himself as a boy and bring back memories of Combray and Doncières. (C I 25–26)

9) The cold weather releases memories of café concerts he used to go to on the first winter evenings and he sings snatches of the popular songs he heard at the time. (C I 69–70)

10) The smell of gasoline reminds him of excursions he took into the country. (C II 558–560)

11) The rain brings back the scent of lilac, and this memory proliferates into others: the sun's rays on the balcony remind him of the pigeons in the Champs-Elysées; the muffling of noise on summer mornings in Paris brings back the taste of cherries; the sound of

the wind and the return of Easter revive his longing for Brittany and Venice. (SCG 86)

12) Tying his scarf, Marcel remembers Albertine. (SCG 159)

13) Badly paved streets leading to the new Guermantes mansion bring back the streets Marcel and Françoise used to take to get to the Champs-Elysées. (PR 181–182)

14) Stumbling on two uneven paving stones in the courtyard of the Guermantes mansion, Marcel recovers his experience of Venice. (PR 191–192)

15) The noise of a spoon rattling against a plate reminds him of a railway worker on a train long ago who was testing the brakes. (PR 192–193)

16) A starched white napkin restores Balbec and the sea. (PR 193–194)

17) The sound of water pipes at the Guermantes' brings back the reality of the marine dining room at Balbec. (PR 199–200)

18) Opening a copy of *François le champi* in the Guermantes' library, his childhood is restored. (PR 210–216)

These memories are not all of the same order. The madeleine-Combray memory is the precursor to the others. The last six memories of *The Past Recaptured* make clear to Marcel the value of involuntary memory in general. The incidents of steeples at Martinville and the trees at Hudimesnil intervene. They are of a special nature. Neither of these "involuntary memories" evokes concrete objects other than themselves, though the three trees might be said to echo the three steeples, for Proust links them together briefly in the text. Even so, the three trees would be a memory of a memory, not the memory of *something*—not recovered sensations that lead to past, real worlds apprehended in the present, in the way the madeleine resurrects Combray from Marcel's unconscious.

Images of trees appear notably twice again. Albertine takes her sketchbooks and disappears into the countryside, roaming among the small towns around Balbec. Marcel follows later in his car. Discussing these experiences, Marcel says:

> Of phantoms pursued, forgotten, sought afresh . . . these Balbec roads were full. When I thought that their trees, pear trees, tamarisks, would outlive me, I seemed to receive from them the warning to set myself to work at last, before the hour should strike of rest everlasting. I left the carriage at Quetteholme. . . . (CP II 218)

And, in a later episode, Marcel is again on a moving conveyance when he makes a similar connection between trees and writing. Coming back to Paris after the war, having spent an unspecified amount of time in a sanatorium, his train stops for a few moments in a clearing. Marcel has given up the idea of becoming a writer, first, because he feels himself incompetent, and second, and worse, because of the "vanity and lie of literature." The last of all his ideals has turned out to be as spurious as all the others:

> ... the train had halted out in the open country. The declining sun shone halfway down the trunks of the trees that lined the railway track. "Trees," thought I to myself, "you have nothing more to say to me; my deadened heart no longer hears you. Behold me in the midst of nature's beauty and yet it is with indifference and ennui that my eyes take note of the line that separates the sun-bathed foliage from the shadowed trunk. If there was once a time when I was able to believe myself a poet, I now know that I am not. . . . If I really had the soul of an artist, what pleasure would I not derive from the sight of that curtain of trees lighted by the declining sun, and in those little flowers growing along the roadbed and raising their heads almost to the step of the railway carriage, so near that I could count their petals, but I shall take good heed not to describe their colour, for who can hope to convey to another a pleasure he has not himself felt? A little later it was with the same indifference that I noted the gold and orange disks with which the same setting sun riddled the windows of a house . . . (PR 177–178)

The steeples of Martinville and the trees of Hudimesnil are not memories at all but premonitions. They contain a hidden future as memories contain a hidden past. This distinction has been made for us on a more human level earlier. On a telephone call from Doncières to Paris, Marcel hears his grandmother's voice and has a premonition of her death. The sweetness of her voice, its isolation from the play of emotions on her face suddenly fills him with the terror of her nonexistence. The separation of the moment must, in the future, be permanent. It is this telephone call that sends him back to Paris to see her. And a year after her death, when he feels he has almost forgotten her, he goes back to the Balbec hotel for his second visit. Bending over to take off his boots—a task his grandmother had performed for him on the very first night they had spent at the hotel—the lost reality of his grandmother wells up inside him, filling his eyes with tears. She has come truly alive for him for the first time since her death. Painfully, her existence within him tells him that they are eternally separated.

The steeples and the trees are precursors of forms that do not yet have a material existence—forms rather than content in the same way that Vinteuil's septet differs from his sonata in the respective hearings of Marcel and Swann. Swann experiences emotions form sets free; Marcel experiences the form as an emotion. The distinction is crucial, for Marcel is an artist and Swann is not.

The steeples and the trees are signposts that hold in precipitation elements that are later to solidify. They contain a specific reality of the future. It will be the writing of *Remembrance of Things Past* in which the process of discovering their meaning will be twofold: in the *writing* of the book as an act, and in the *content* of the book which explains how that act came into being. The essay Marcel wrote on the steeples of Martinville and left in the hamper of Dr. Percepied's carriage is to be brought out and expanded. The steeples and the trees are secret knowledge that Marcel cannot bring to life, though he glimpses the secret and the way to discover it almost simultaneously. At the time, that glimpse is not yet the revelation it will become. Just as he contains lost time within himself, so the steeples and the trees are vessels of concealment; their confined messages will be released only when Marcel understands the true nature of his vocation. They are postdated numens. Marcel experiences on each of these occasions something he does not yet consciously know and which does not yet exist—his book, which is his life—nonexistent in fact but buried within himself.

The steeples and the trees burst open in light. As they gallop away and toward him, his book is still germinating in the dark.

VI

THE WAY

> . . . *the only true paradise is always the paradise we have lost* . . . (PR 195)

On a visit to Tansonville to spend some time with Gilberte, now Mme. de Saint-Loup, Marcel finds the early scenes of his childhood unevocative, without poetry or savor. The past is a dead crumb, the present listless, the future a predictable series of stale repetitions. By the time Marcel attends the final party at the Princesse de Guermantes', life has proved to be hopeless. Like Swann, he has led a fruitless pilgrimage. He has survived the destructiveness of love, the blandishments of society—but to what purpose? Even literature seems false, the desire for immortality vain, in both senses. The only future event of significance on his calendar is his own death.

Two kinds of revelation await him. The first is literary. Going through an unpublished diary of the Goncourts' (the text of this is a Goncourt parody-pastiche concocted by Proust), he comes upon a description of the Verdurin "clan." It is naïve and journalistic, but, like the steeples and the trees, has an important secret message. Even lives as stupid and shallow as the Verdurins' can be recorded and add something to the storehouse of posterity. It is from Saint-Simon, after all, that Marcel has learned of life at Versailles. Moreover, reading these social mirrorings of life, he becomes aware of underlying truths that do not seem to be available to the Goncourts. Marcel holds these truths within himself; he does not yet know they are usable.

Further revelations are to come, and they are the most important moments, thematically, in Proust's novel. At the climactic apex of his book, he has a series of involuntary memories that flood into his being at the Guermantes' final party. The whole cast is about to be brought onstage, rattling with death. Were it not for the experience Marcel undergoes just prior to and during it, he would simply be another skeleton delivering his funeral oration in a spray of gossip.

The first involuntary memory occurs while Marcel is again in motion and in a carriage. The streets leading to the Guermantes' mansion disappear; he has the sensation that he is going to the Champs-Elysées with Françoise. Those past streets crowd out the present ones. Getting out of the carriage in the courtyard, he stumbles on two uneven paving stones. His body is electrified by a former self; the uneven paving stones restore Venice, the sensibility that experienced Venice. The sensation that he had once felt stepping on two uneven slabs in the Baptistry of St. Mark, repeated in this moment, selects the Venice days out of the decades of time. Entering a boudoir-library to await the conclusion of a piece of music that is being played, he hears a spoon knock against a plate carried by a servant. Marcel instantly becomes aware of a former experience submerging the present—the sound of the hammer of a railway worker who once long ago tested the brakes on a train Marcel was riding to Paris. The train had stopped in a clearing. This sound evokes the following:

> The same kind of felicity as I had received from the uneven paving stones now came over me . . . what seemed to me so delightful was the very row of trees which I had found it wearisome to study and describe . . . (PR 192–193)

A waiter brings some cakes and a glass of orangeade to Marcel in the library. Wiping his mouth with a napkin, its starched whiteness brings back what seems his entire knowledge of Balbec and the sea. The napkin has exactly the same kind of starchiness as the one with which he had attempted to dry himself before the window the first day of his arrival at Balbec. Within its folds, a green-blue ocean spreads its plumage like a peacock tail. Soon after, the sound of water pipes makes the entire dining room of the Balbec hotel rise up from the past. And, opening a copy of *François le champi* in the library, the very book his mother read to him while he was falling asleep in his Combray bedroom, his childhood is revived.

An important undercurrent ties these involuntary memories together. They are all memories of journeys or places. The very distinction Marcel made earlier between "the name" and "the place" is here proved true on an entirely different level. We see now why a particular class of involuntary memories occurred while Marcel was in motion. Each was transfigured by the velocity of the future. Places—Combray, Balbec, Doncières, Paris, and Venice—are no longer to be found on any meaningful map except the one waiting to be unfurled within Marcel. These extratemporal moments are true revelations and offer us a profound sense of renewal simply because they have been experienced before. The only true paradise is always the paradise we have lost. Time lost is about to be regained in the writing of the novel. The sparks along the internal, wired connections of his nerves can be used to rekindle all the worlds they have ever lit:

> But when from a long-distant past nothing subsists, after the people are dead, after the things are broken and scattered, still, alone, more fragile, but with more vitality, more unsubstantial, more persistent, more faithful, the smell and taste of things remain poised a long time, like souls . . . and bear unfaltering, in the tiny and almost impalpable drops of their essence, the vast structure of recollection. (SW 65)

We have just read, of course, the very work Marcel is about to undertake. Like *Finnegans Wake, Remembrance of Things Past* is its own self-sealing device. Circular in structure, its end leads us back to its beginning. The word "time" embedded in the first sentence of the book rings out grandly as the last word of the novel and brings us once again to where we started. The circle is not on a plane but exists in three—or to be true to Proust's intentions, four—dimensions. His novel is architectural rather than linear, like the church of Saint Hilaire at Combray which, conquering location by physical mass, derives its energy from the epochs of time that have seeped into its very cells. The material church, absorbing time, can no longer be divorced from it. Proust's book is such a monument. Time is a substance as well as a process and all things are immersed in it.

Memory exists outside of time. The beautiful girls at Balbec are not necessarily the hideous, fat dowagers across the room, made monstrous by the years. Their youth dwells, as does our own, within ourselves. It has merely to be recaptured from time where it exists as an eternal moment.

The regaining of time is the true quest of mankind. An instant freed from the order of time in the individual is man liberated from the same order. Time, more deceptive even than memory, can prevent us from knowing this. We assume chronology is succession. The young Marcel waiting in his bedroom for his mother to kiss him good night might easily have been forgotten. Yet, as Proust shows us, he holds the magic lantern that illuminates everything.

We are taken back to Combray at this final party by means other than memory. Marcel meets, for the first time, Mlle. de Saint-Loup, the daughter of Gilberte and Saint-Loup. She embodies the two early landscapes of himself. On his visit to Tansonville to see Gilberte, Marcel has had an inkling of this. He discovers in old age that by taking a shortcut it is possible to get from Swann's way to the Guermantes way. The separated kingdoms of his boyhood were a united empire always. In the person of Mlle. de Saint-Loup, Swann's way and the Guermantes way become one.

Marcel exhausts more than the illusions of love and society; he exhausts the illusion of personality. It is one thing to see that the physical surface of people and things is a delusion; it is quite another to see that, beyond the outwardly perceptible, we come upon a world equally illusory. Nothing exists until it is connected by memory to a former experience; the connection between two nonrealities gives them an existence. A starched napkin has no meaning in itself; Balbec and the sea are forgettable. In the linkage of the two, Balbec and the sea are resurrected.

Love is a disease of the ideal but of enormous value because it informs us of the ideal. Without Albertine, there would be no *Remembrance of Things Past*. Similarly, sensation is valuable though mortal. It leads us to where immortality may be. Only intelligence is under attack in Proust as a mode of perception. But as only those people who have loved can speak of it as a delusion with authority, it is only through intelligence that one has the privilege of categorizing it. Explaining everything, Proust creates a universe that does not exclude the inexplicable.

Proust is the greatest of disenchanters. But only because he was so greatly enchanted. *Remembrance of Things Past* is a gigantic disappearing act in which the magician vanishes along with his magic in the service of illusion. He does so to prove to us that the illusory is real. By the time we reach the end of *Remembrance of Things Past*, Swann and the Duchesse de Guermantes, upon whom so much time and elucidation have been expended, are revealed at last for what they are. Two human beings in the boyhood of Marcel Proust he once conceived of as gods. Now the true god, the writer, paying homage to the deities of his childhood, secreting their lives from within himself, confers upon them a genuine immortality.

Printed in the USA
CPSIA information can be obtained
at www.ICGtesting.com
JSHW022146081024
71285JS00001B/6

9 781589 880795